NEW YORK ENCOUNTER

This booklet contains transcripts, not reviewed by the speakers, of talks given at New York Encounter 2014

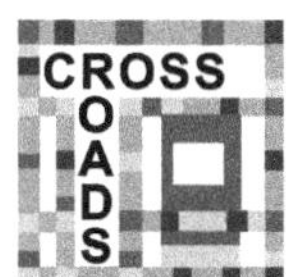

Crossroads Cultural Center

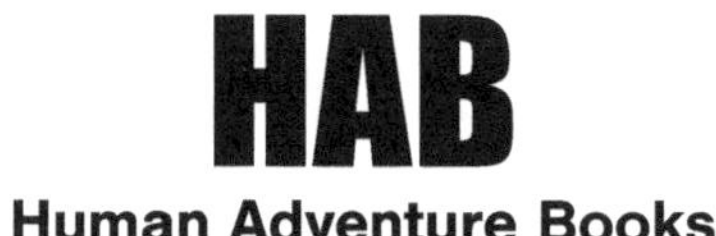

Human Adventure Books

The Time of the Person
Proceedings of New York Encounter 2014
Crossroads Cultural Center

ISBN: 978-1-941457-00-9

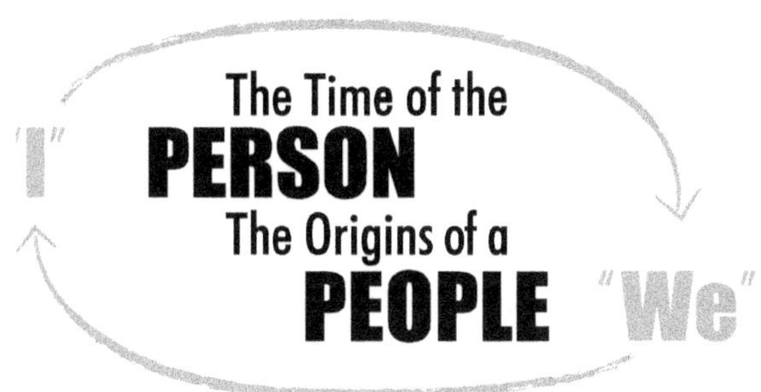

We live in a time of uncertainty. We like to think that we live in a peaceful, ordered society, but again and again we have discovered that the darkness of blind violence can envelop us at any time, like in Newtown or in Boston. We take comfort in our general prosperity, but we have an uneasy feeling that the current economic crisis, with its high unemployment rate, is different from others in the past, and that things may get worse rather than better. We cherish our freedom, but we worry about the manipulation of democracy by powerful, apparently invincible forces. Such uncertainty seems to cast a cynical doubt on the ideals that define a human culture: the exaltation of the person, the pursuit of happiness, the commitment to build, and the pride of belonging to a people.

How can we fight back?

"When...the grip of a hostile society tightens around us to the point of threatening the vivacity of our expression, and when a cultural and social hegemony tends to penetrate the heart, stirring up our already natural uncertainties, then **the time of the person has come.**"
(Msgr. Luigi Giussani)

What is the person? Who are we, really? What do we cry out for? Who can answer?

New York Encounter 2014 explored the nature of the person and the flourishing of that person in belonging to a people.

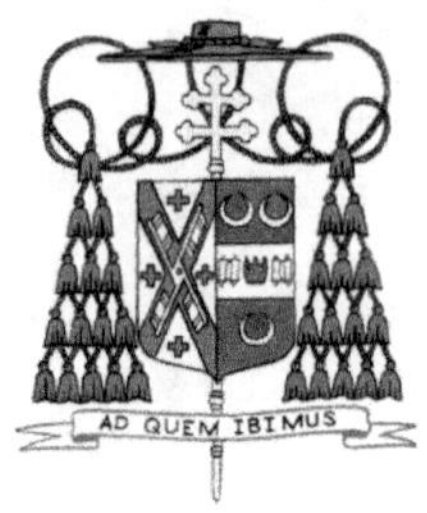

OFFICE OF THE CARDINAL
1011 FIRST AVENUE
NEW YORK, NY 10022

January 17, 2014

Dear Friends in the Lord:

It is a joy and an honor to welcome you to the *New York Encounter,* organized by Communion and Liberation and the Crossroads Cultural Center.

As the Archbishop of New York, I believe it is most fitting to hold this public cultural festival held here in what Blessed – soon to be Saint – Pope John Paul II called "the capital of the world." The *New York Encounter* will help to promote a society of truth and love through its many conferences, discussions, live artistic performances, and exhibits. Your focus on the nature of the human person, and the flourishing of the human person in belonging to a people, is very much in keeping with Pope Francis's exhortation that, "it is vitally important for the Church today to go forth and preach the Gospel to all: to all places, on all occasions, without hesitation, reluctance or fear. The joy of the Gospel is for all people: no one can be excluded." (Evangelii Gaudium, 23)

Please permit me to extend a special word of welcome to His Eminence, Cardinal Sean O'Malley, and to our Nuncio, Archbishop Carlo Maria Vigano, who are just two of the outstanding speakers who will be with you this weekend. You will all have a special place in my Masses and prayers this weekend for a fruitful and enriching *Encounter.*

Faithfully in Christ,

Timothy Michael Cardinal Dolan
Archbishop of New York

Index

"Life Belongs to Something Greater" (Msgr. Luigi Giussani)
Msgr. Lorenzo Albacete, Fr. Samir Khalil Samir,
and Mr. Frank Simmonds 7

Hoping Against Hope
Fr. Samir Khalil Samir, SJ 23

Is It Possible to Work this Way?
Dr. Michael Naughton and Mr. Bernhard Scholz 35

Lost?
Fr. José Medina and Dr. Pedro Noguera 55

That Hidden Companionship: Stronger than Loneliness
Dr. Fabrice Hadjadj and Dr. David Schindler 75

"Go Out, Head for the Periphery" (Pope Francis)
Cardinal Seán O'Malley and Msgr. Lorenzo Albacete 95

Abraham: The Birth of the "I," the Birth of a People
Dr. David Flatto and Fr. Richard Veras 115

From "I" to "We": The Time of the Person, The Origins of a People
Fr. Peter John Cameron and Fr. Julián Carrón 133

Introduction to the Exhibit: "The Face of Jesus: From that Gaze, the Human Person"
by Cardinal Seán O'Malley, OFM Cap. 149

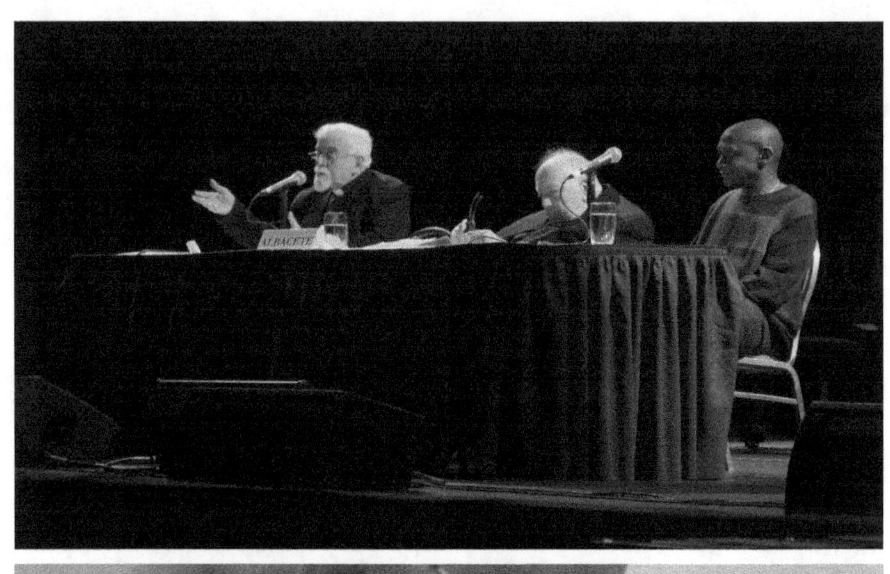
ALBACETE

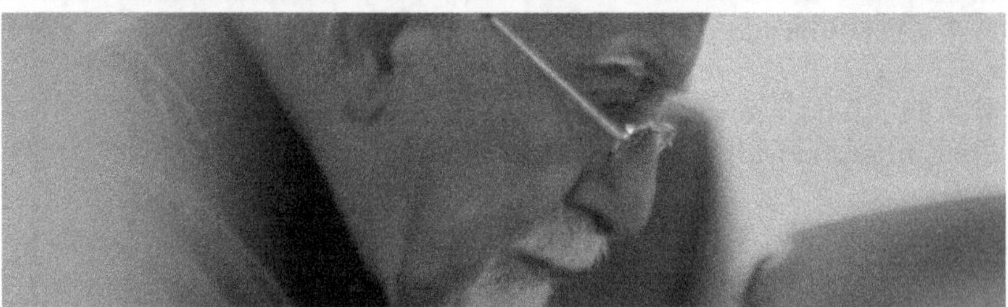

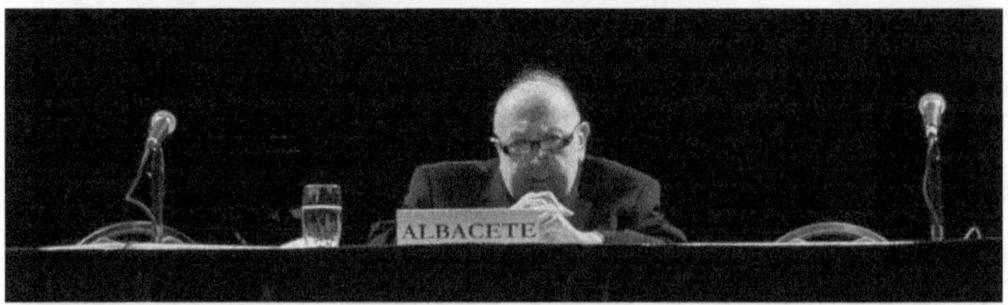
ALBACETE

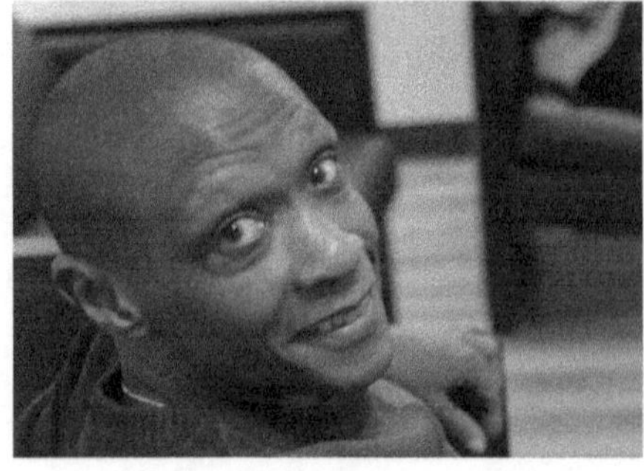

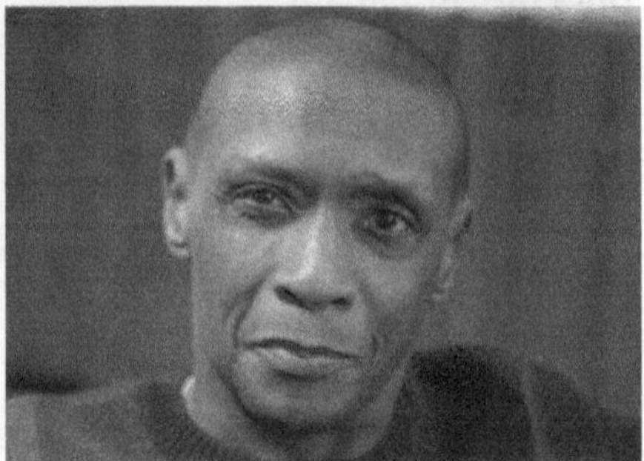

"Life Belongs to Something Greater" (Msgr. Luigi Giussani)

Msgr. Lorenzo Albacete,[1] Fr. Samir Khalil Samir, SJ,[2] and Mr. Frank Simmonds[3]

Introduction

"For me the important thing is to reawaken the evidence that our own life is not born from itself, it does not have itself as destiny, but it belongs to something bigger, and it is this bigger thing that constitutes us [...] Something bigger constitutes us. In other words, the discovery of the paradox that I am Another. I cannot say 'I' unless I say 'You, unless I say 'You who make me.' And I affirm this when I try to explain what prayer is. Jesus said: 'The whole world is settled in the lie,' and nowadays the lie has become completely paroxysmal because the concreteness of life has been erased; but the place where the lie operates is the person. In fact, you kill yourself or you live like someone who is dead, accepting to be dead; and this is the real suicide. Therefore, it is once again in the person that the recovery, the rebirth, the revolution takes place. How does this recovery happen at the present time? This is the question we face. Externally, the only answer is that we have an encounter with a presence that is different; that we bump into a different presence; and this presence, then, can act as a reagent, as a catalyst of energies that up till now were absconding."

(Luigi Giussani, translation from *Il senso della nascita,* Rizzoli)

Friday, January 17, 2014

[1]Theologian

[2]Professor of Islamic Studies, University of Saint Joseph, Beirut

[3]Doorman

"Life Belongs to Something Greater" (Msgr. Luigi Giussani)

"Choruses from 'The Rock,'" by T.S. Eliot.

The Eagle soars in the summit of Heaven,
The Hunter with his dogs pursues his circuit.
O perpetual revolution of configured stars,
O perpetual recurrence of determined seasons,
O world of spring and autumn, birth and dying!
The endless cycle of idea and action,
Endless invention, endless experiment,
Brings knowledge of motion, but not of stillness;
Knowledge of speech, but not of silence;
Knowledge of words, and ignorance of the Word.

All our knowledge brings us nearer to our ignorance,
All our ignorance brings us nearer to death,
But nearness to death, no nearer to GOD.
Where is the Life we have lost in living?
Where is the wisdom we have lost in knowledge?
Where is the knowledge we have lost in information?
The cycles of Heaven in twenty centuries
Bring us farther from GOD and nearer to the Dust...

...What life have you if you have not life together?
There is no life that is not in community,
And no community not lived in praise of God.
Even the anchorite who meditates alone,
For whom the days and nights repeat the praise of God,
Prays for the Church, the Body of Christ incarnate.
And now you live dispersed on ribbon roads.
And no man knows or cares who is his neighbour
Unless his neighbour makes too much disturbance,
But all dash to and fro in motor cars,
Familiar with the roads and settled nowhere.
Nor does the family even move about together.
But every son would have his motor cycle,
And daughters ride away on casual pillions.
Much to cast down, much to build, much to restore;

Let the work not delay, time and the arm not waste;
Let the clay be dug from the pit, let the saw cut the stone.
Let the fire not be quenched in the forge...

...O weariness of men who turn from God
To the grandeur of your mind and the glory of your action,
To arts and inventions and daring enterprises.
To schemes of human greatness thoroughly discredited.
Binding the earth and the water to your service,
Exploiting the seas and developing the mountains,

Dividing the stars into common and preferred.
Engaged in devising the perfect refrigerator,
Engaged in working out a rational morality,
Engaged in printing as many books as possible,
Plotting of happiness and flinging empty bottles,
Turning from your vacancy to fevered enthusiasm
For nation or race or what you call humanity;
Though you forget the way to the Temple,
There is one who remembers the way to your door...

...Men! polish your teeth on rising and retiring;
Women! polish your fingernails:
You polish the tooth of the dog and the talon of the cat.
Why should men love the Church? Why should they love her laws?
She tells them of Life and Death, and of all that they would forget.
She is tender where they would be hard, and hard where they like to be soft.
She tells them of Evil and Sin, and other unpleasant facts.
They constantly try to escape
From the darkness outside and within
By dreaming of systems so perfect that no one will need to be good.
But the man that is will shadow
The man that pretends to be.

❖ ❖ ❖ ❖ ❖

Albacete: The reading of *Choruses from 'The Rock,'* by T.S. Eliot, was given by Tony Hendra.

Hearing that Tony was going to be here and read to us, I suddenly realized what would be a good theme for my presentation. And it is a single scripture passage, which I have here.

"My brother Esau is a hairy man, but I am a smooth man." My brother Esau is a hairy man, but I am a smooth man. That is the passage upon which I will base my talk this evening, in an attempt to explain why we chose the theme for this year, which is the task given to me. Fr. Giussani used to say that my participation in his charism consisted in my ability to vulgarize its teaching, so I'm hauled out whenever the title appears a little bit difficult. Because frankly, what the heck *is* the "time of the person," and what does it have to do with "the time of the people"? Well, it's all found in "My brother is a hairy man, but I am a smooth man."

The time of the person. You are here tonight, and I venture to say that for you, for me, for all of us here, something is worrying us. I mean, beyond the usual worries of getting through the day there is a deeper unrest. That's the word: *unrest*. In this unrest we seek a source that will restore a direction to our lives, that will give us a clarity that will guide us through this unrest.

Fr. Giussani describes the unrest in these words. "When the grip of a hostile society tightens around us to the point of threatening the vivacity of our expression, and when a cultural and social hegemony tends to penetrate the heart, stirring up our already natural uncertainties"—I love that term, by the way: *natural uncertainties*—"then when that happens," he says, "the time of the person has come."

It's an amazing thing. I don't think a description of the current cultural instability is difficult to find, or to confirm, unless we're hiding somewhere under the water of the sea. It's in the air that we breathe. There is a search. We try to hang on to the ideology of modernity as a way of living our humanity decently, and yet at the same time there is dissatisfaction. It's a tension that in my own life I sometimes find intolerable. If this becomes not only a private way of thinking but a societal one, if the whole culture is built on this uncertainty, then we've got a problem. What to do about it? Well, some people suggest we attempt to escape this situation of the ruling uncertainty. I don't know where they intend to escape to, but I can sympathize with the desire to just hide from plagues. That's why I love those psalms which speak of being taken up to a mountain by an eagle or something and being protected there from the raging seas. Protection is comforting, but I don't find it in my daily life.

So I don't think escape is the solution. As far as Christians are concerned, I remember a few years ago reading an article in *Time* or *Newsweek* that a popular Evangelical Christian leader—he had a huge following, like you would later find in some of those megachurches—was saying it was time for Christians to withdraw from American society. Start our own schools, our own hospitals, etc. And there was a big discussion about it. But Fr. Giussani's response to this cultural situation is not that. In fact, it is the very antithesis of disengagement and escape.

Yet some people urge the opposite: stay and fight. From the League of Weapons to actual weapons, we've seen fighting even in the name of Christ. Well, of course that, too, is rejected by Fr. Giussani. Then what are we to do if not escape or stay and fight? What do we do, become resigned to it? And that, by the way, is another response embraced by still other people: "Who cares? You know, be resigned to it, it's all hopeless." So it's all hopeless, or let's stay and fight, or let's run away from it. None of those are adequate responses.

Here, this weekend at the New York Encounter, we will hear not many lectures but many witnesses: people who will tell us what they've done in response to this cultural situation. The time of the person.

Let's look at it this way: what this way of thinking, where it springs from, where our cultural vision and action spring from, is the experience of our awareness of being a person; of being, that is, some*one* and not just some*thing*.

If we are someone, we are also something, so that is no problem. The problem is how to move from being just some*thing* to some*one*. I don't know whether it is so easy to give a theoretical answer to that. But I cannot, I refuse, even in the circles of utmost uncertainty—I refuse to acknowledge someone who says, definitively, that he or she is just something, and that someones don't exist. I've never met such a person. All of that may be covered up by many confusing ways of thinking and speaking, but it's there. The unrest is there. And if you begin to move your heart to that point, which is the source of this culture and of any culture—the being someone—as you move to that, the unrest increases. I know many people—and I really do mean many—who have begun the path, the pilgrimage to that ground zero, and as they approach it they get more and more scared and just leave the path, just leave it.

I used to attend meetings with friends of mine to discuss this situation, to try to approach it from the other side, to try to appreciate the positive ways in which the modern culture teaches us. And we could start with that, no problem. In fact, one prefers that to starting with depressing things. "Oh, it's all over, man, we're all sinking." Forget it. You know, one thing that I admire today, however falsely it is pursued, is the insistence on freedom. For long time in the history of humankind, an insistence on freedom didn't even concern anyone. That's a progress made, because the experience of freedom lies at the very heart of what we're looking for, at the very source of our person. Only persons are free. If there is freedom, only persons can experience it. So you can start an exploration, a dialogue, with the question of freedom, and if you start positively, it's no problem. We can continue. We used to do that, and were able to actually begin to approach the Mystery with a capital M—the fact that doesn't end, the Mystery where this is found—within which this point, this opening to personhood is found.

And as we approached that point, suddenly someone would say, "Let's get Chinese food." Now, I love Chinese food. And I would rather be sitting down having some of it right now, actually. But you know, it's even funny, yet we're not aware that it's funny. What is this, when you say I am a person, I am free or I want to be free, I have these rights—to what experience are you giving this name? What is it that has touched you? I would propose to you what Fr. Giussani would answer: what has touched you is the experience of Someone else, of an Other with a capital O, that opens you up to have a relationship with you.

As we are filled up with the life of this Other, we experience our personhood more and more strongly. You may be lying down on your death bed, weak in all aspects of your body, yet inside you may be stronger than ever. I'm working on my canonization, but haven't gotten there yet. Anyway, I'm not asking you to be spiritual about this.

There is something about human experience. If we just look at it and see what the stuff of personhood is made of, and we grab it and allow ourselves to be fulfilled by it and love it—to that degree we are strong, strong to resist the ideologies, because what the ideologies attack is the experience of being a person. The response is simple: let's be a person. Let's give a witness of what a person really is in life—to everyone, without running away, without evading anything. A testimony. This has happened to me. You can tell in a person's face and eyes and gestures that something has happened. That is what Fr. Giussani says. This is the time of the person, and we have devoted this weekend to examples of what it means to live in this time of the person. It's a relationship experience. It's a relationship of belonging to a reality that unites us all, and it's in the experience of belonging to this common reality that we find the birth of a people.

Samir: I am Ben Samir Khalil Samir, born in Cairo, Egypt. I work mainly in Lebanon now but also teach in different European countries. I would like to tell you something about my experience with Muslim friends, and with Muslims in general. Egypt is around 10% Christian, 90% Muslim. We Christians are the original community. The word "Copts," used to designate the Christians of Egypt, is pronounced "gipty" in Arabic, and comes from "Egypt," "Egyptians." So we know we are the Egyptians. The Muslims came in the seventh century and later on, and joined us. But they became the majority. First the Christians, then the Muslims; and we are a family. We lived like that often but not always. We occasionally had some hard times in the Middle Ages, in the 14th and 15th centuries. In the modern times since the '60s, however, it's become difficult for Christians—more difficult than it was before God put us in this country. But we are one nation, one family. The question is: Why are we here? Do we have a mission? Certainly if we are believers, we have a mission. God put us in this country to be testimonies of the Gospel in the middle of our brother Muslims.

Usually, I had very positive experiences with the Muslims. I'll give you some examples of what I lived. In the '70s, I started working in Upper Egypt, in the southern villages, to develop the country socially and at the educational level. We were a group of Christians very much involved in this work in Upper Egypt; young people. Though I was young at the time, I was the oldest one, more or less. One particular friend was Muslim and wanted to work with us: I remember going to the very south of Egypt with him and others in a pickup truck. It was a hard day. We were twelve persons with conflicts between us, human conflicts, and personalities that were not perfectly in accord with each other. By midnight, we had nearly reached Akhmim, our destination village. My friend Mamoud, the Muslim, came from behind the pickup—I was sitting in the front—and he says, "Fr. Samir, I think we've had a hard day, with a lot of conflicts. I think we need to pray together." I said, "Well, it's beautiful, why not?"

"Yes. When we arrive, I suggest that we celebrate Mass." Keep in mind he was the only Muslim. I said, "But you know it's almost midnight and we still have half an hour to go. Do you think we are ready for that? Ask the others." So in the pickup he repeated, "I propose that we pray together and celebrate Mass." They said, "Okay," and we made reconciliation.

Then later, in 2000, I was teaching at the Institute for Muslim-Christian Studies in Beirut. Half of the students were Muslims and half were Christians. I tried to explain from one side the Koran and Muslim tradition, and from the other side the Gospel and Christian tradition. At one point the Muslim students said, "We cannot accept this approach to human rights, because in the Koran there are some points which are against this." I was teaching with a Muslim professor, by the way; all the courses were given together by two instructors. And the Muslim professor said, "Look, what the Koran is saying, if we take it literally, cannot be applied today. But if we interpret it... For instance, the Koran says we must cut the thief's hand. This was the only possibility back then. But today there are other possibilities to educate someone to help him not to steal." The student responded:

"But in the Koran it is clearly said. So we have to do it." Then I offered the following: "We have also in the Bible, in the Hebrew Bible, chapters and verses that deal very harshly with thieves, with adulterers—also violent verses. But we are trying to interpret them, to see what they mean. We take the meaning, and we see what we can do today." We had a discussion, and at the end the conclusion was: we have to rethink our faith from both sides, and help each other reinterpret it.

Two years later, one of the students—he was from the Shia community, the more minority community—came to me and said, "Fr. Samir, I would like you to be my spiritual father." The phrase "spiritual father" is totally unknown to Muslims in Arabic. I said, "But how can I do it? I am Christian, I don't want to Christianize you." He said, "No, no. I want you to be my guide spiritually." And so he came twice a month to discuss his problems with me, and I tried to answer, to give some advice, from the Bible and from the Koran, from something possibly found in both. This was in 2000.

Last year, the same student was in London as the chief of the Shia community there, recognized as such by the British government. He came to me and said, "You remember me?" And I said, "Certainly, yeah." "You were my spiritual father. Now I would like you to come with me. I invite you to Iran, through Iraq first, to see the holy place, Najaf, and to talk with the Shia imam there." I said, "But it's not the right time," and so on. I had genuinely practical problems. He said, "Please, come. I spoke with Sistani." Sistani is the highest authority in the Shia community, both in Iraq and Iran. "And he is waiting for you." So my student friend prepared everything. He gave me the ticket and the visa, and we went. It was a three-day conference and there were hundreds of imams. They invited me to open the session with a word, a brief talk. And since the Koran begins with the expression, "In the name of God the Merciful, the All-merciful," I started my talk by quoting that sentence. Then I went further, quoting the Beatitudes: "Happy are the merciful, for they will receive mercy; happy are the..." and so on. I developed the theme of mercy, noting that mercy also means to forgive, and that forgiveness is more than love. At the end, they came and said, "We are the same. Christians and Muslims see God as the Merciful." I tried to add something, saying, "Yes, but He is also Father. This does not mean, as you usually say, there are three Gods, because fatherhood is something spiritual, and not limited to the one who physically generates."

Two weeks later, the same Imam Weisan came to me and said, "Now, we are invited to go to the holy city of Quom in Iran, and I will bring you the ticket and the visa and everything. We are invited to spend the week there." So I went. It was almost Christmas, something incredible. I spent eight days in Quom, the holy city of the Shia, passing each day with approximately 20 imams, seeing what they were doing. We became such good friends that on the last day they said, "You have to give us a conference on the dialogue between Muslims and Christians, and how we are all brothers." There were 70 Imams present. I spoke in Arabic because imams understand Arabic.

These experiences show how close we could be. At the same time, we know that there are confrontations, very strong confrontations, in Egypt, Syria, and Lebanon. In Lebanon we had 15 years of war between Christians and Muslims. Both are there. The question is: Why do we struggle so strongly against each other?

Why are there so many radical Muslims—maybe 10% of the total population—in our days? We see it everywhere, not only in the Middle East but also in other countries like Pakistan, a little bit in Bangladesh, Afghanistan, even in Malaysia and Indonesia. Something is changing in the world, and not for the better. But what is certain is that we can live together as brothers. Two years ago in Cairo and elsewhere, we had what we call the Arab Spring. When the Muslim Brotherhood came and introduced themselves into this movement, and tried to say we have to apply the Sharia, we have to be true Muslims—the youth answered, "We are all believers, whether we are Muslims or Christians. We all believe in God. Please, let us live our faith as we want. Don't oblige us to do this and that. We are believers. We want to remain believers."

This feeling was common to Christians and Muslims. They were asking for liberty of belief. They were not abandoning the faith, but were asking for the practice of the faith according to their spiritual feeling. This is the trend now. And the confrontation you heard about with the Muslim Brotherhood, with President Morsi, was centered precisely on this point.

We don't want you to impose your Islam on us. We could say the same for Christianity. Let us live it freely. Give us good advice, and leave us to practice it as we think best. Today, it's a chance for the Middle East and for the Muslim world. It's a chance for the Christian world.

Now the final question for me is why God puts us Christians in the Muslim countries of the Middle East. We have a mission, just as you have a mission here. Your world in the West is more and more a secularized world. The moral values, the ethical values, are often put aside. We have to give testimony that this does not enlarge our humanity, this is not the true freedom, but probably makes us less human. We want to be the true humanists: Christian humanists, Muslim humanists. Believers who affirm that man is created by God, is coming from God, and will return to God. To change this world, to build the world of justice and dignity and fraternity—this is also our task in the Muslim world: to build together. The word *together* is the essential word. To build together the city, the society of believers open to others, believers who identify first with the poor, with those who are under pressure. Those are our first brothers, whether they are Muslims, Christians, Jews, or unbelievers. They are free to think what they want, but still we are one family. This is our mission. That's why immigration is for us a great temptation, to come to the West and live in a better way, in a more just way. But we have to remain in our area, to change this world and make it more open to everyone, more just.

This is my experience, and this is the last word: it's possible. I experienced it, and I am now 76. I can say that since my youth in school—it was a Christian school, but 35% Muslim—since my youth and until today, I experienced daily that if we want we can live together in love. This is not more difficult: it's more difficult to live with hate, it's easier to live with love. We just have to look at the other as Jesus looked at each person in Jerusalem, in Palestine, in Nazareth, Capurnaum, His city, everywhere. I know that this is your aim, being followers of Don Giussani. This is our aim for all of us, Christians and non-Christians. And I pray with you to God that we remain truthful to our vocation of testifying to God's love for humanity, which is the testimony of the Gospel. Because God loved the world so much that He came Himself through His Son Jesus, and sent us the Holy Spirit, which is God, to our hearts.

Albacete: Mr. Frank Simmonds was born in Brooklyn, New York, and grew up on Long Island. His parents were West Indian, from the St. Thomas Virgin islands—and that's a very good region to be from. They raised him in the Roman Catholic faith. His mother died of cancer when he was 17 years old, and for the next 25 years Frank fell farther and farther from his faith. He followed an alternative lifestyle of drug addiction, homelessness, crime and incarceration—until he encountered the Power much greater than all his mistakes, the Power that enabled him to accept the change in his life. Frank has lived in that encounter ever since. He once again resides in Brooklyn, with his wife and two young sons, and works here in Manhattan as a doorman.

Simmonds: By the way, Msgr. Albacete married me and my wife, so we're kind of close. But as the first of many things, I want to say that I have joy today. Today is so beautiful. It's beyond description. But one thing I must acknowledge is that it is not generated by me.

I was brought up Roman Catholic, so I knew all about God and everything, but to be honest with you the true love of my life was my mom. Her love was so unconditional. I'd never experienced it apart from her presence. So, subsequently, you know when you put all your eggs in one basket, you realize at times that things can be taken away from you. And when she died, I felt that unconditional love was gone.

To say that I was hurt is an understatement, but who was I to blame? God is a good choice. He created everybody, He's so merciful and everything. He took out of my life the one I loved the most. How could this be? "You got the power," I said to Him. "You could have kept her. You could have brought her back." So yeah, I chose to do things my way, like Frank Sinatra used to sing: "I did it my way." I went out and did a lot of drugs, lost everything that my mother had worked for, the house, the home. Some people say, "Where was your father?" He took off and went his own way. And I lost everything. But you know, I just went on because I didn't care. If I killed myself or something, the worst thing that could happen is I'd end up with my mom. That's the crazy thinking you go through, you know, when you're really suffering; sometimes you lose your mind. I was of those people who lost track of everything. So I wanted to take control of my life. I didn't need God to control it. Look what He did—He took my mother from me. For me, at that moment, God was just as good as a picture on the wall.

So I took control of my life, thinking that I could do better. I spiraled down through so many different things. But I refused, I refused to acknowledge that He existed. I still wanted to do it my way, so much so that one night, after selling my coat and my shoes, I sat on the steps of an abandoned building. I'd run out of money, had nothing to get any more drugs with, and I said, "Well, I'll rob the next guy who comes by, and then I'll just keep moving. I'll get another pair of shoes, another..."—you know. It's two o'clock in the morning, so of course you're not expecting a whole bunch of people running by that you can rob. But I hear footsteps and am like, "Oh, good." I look around and here's this guy, just doe-dee-doe, coming up the sidewalk. I thought, *Perfect, I got it.* As he came closer, I noticed he was wearing black and he had something white by his neck. And I was like, *Oh man, this is really getting bad now. I'm about to rob a priest! Dag, man, how low can you go?*

I'm telling you this because the only way I can communicate to you is through experience, not my intellect. I'm not all that smart of a guy, but I can paint this picture because I experienced it. That's something that sticks. So anyway, he comes by, and he gets closer, and I'm preparing myself, getting all rigid. Six foot one, a hundred thirty-five pounds, and now I want to go rob people on the street. *All right, we'll do it, we'll make it happen.* Anyway, he gets closer and I think, *You know what, let me give him a break. If he don't say nothing to me, I'm going to let him go. I'll find another guy.* He goes by, doe-dee-doe, and he stops right at the corner and I'm like, *Here goes.* But he turns around and says, "Young man, if you think God is going to come and lay down with you in the gutter, He won't. You know why? Because He's holy. But if you ask Him, He'll come and take you out of this gutter." And I said, "Man, you got to get stepping, because I'm ready to jump on you right now, man, you know what I mean? Go!" As he went up the street and turned the corner, I thought, *Forget it, I'm going to rob him.*

I went running around the corner but he was gone. I looked. There were no lights on. He was gone, and it tortured me, it tortured me so bad I felt...I don't know, I can't explain the words for it. Here we are now talking about the time of the person and people—I didn't even think I was a person then. I didn't even know what a person was. I don't even think I knew what love was. I didn't even love myself. So I was tortured, and tortured, and tortured. I was one of those guys you see walking up the street. And I said, *You know, I can't take this.* It was like one of those Wolfman movies: the full moon comes up, I turn into this monster. But when do I turn back into me? I'm the monster all the time. I couldn't take it.

I wanted to end it. I come up with brilliant ideas when I think by myself: suicide! *Hey, yeah, that'll put an end to everything.* All of sudden, I got all these great plans of how I'm going to commit suicide: I'm going to go to the train station and jump in front of a train. Brilliant! With my luck, it would cut off my arms and legs and my body would still be there alive, you know. This is the way my life was. But I was going to do this brilliant thing. And as I was walking up the street I was yelling at God, "You're not real! You're not real! You're not real! You're that picture on the wall. Let me see you stop me from what I'm about to do right now. You know, you're all that powerful, you're...stop me!" And as I was walking—I can't believe this—something cried out from inside of me. It cried out and it came of my mouth and it said, "God, if you stop me from what I'm about to do, I will serve you for the rest of my life." And I was like, *What?! What is this?!* I couldn't believe it, my skin started to crawl. This is not some abstract thing that's happening, this is something real, as real as I can possibly experience something.

After that happened, I was in such shock. I'm standing in the middle of the street, a car was going by and a guy yells, "Yo, man, get out of the street!" I was like, *Man, maybe he'll hit me and I can get it done without having to do all the work myself.* But he just went on by. Before I got to the train station, I thought of the guy from the night before, the priest. And I thought of what he told me. He said, "Look, if you really get into real deep trouble, call this number." It was *1-800-WeDetox* or something. And, just so conveniently, there was a phone there. I went to the phone and dialed the toll-free number. They were like, "Yes." I said, "What are you saying Yes to me for, I need the answers from you." They said, "What answer are you looking for?" I said, "Man, I'm a drug addict, really hopeless. I don't know why I'm making this phone call, but I'm about to kill myself. Help me."

They asked me where I was and then picked me up. They took me to a hospital that was like a rehab. I said, "This hospital looks familiar." "Yeah," they said, "this used to be Hempstead General Hospital." I was in shock: Hempstead General Hospital was where my dead mother had worked. And I realized, right then and there, that someone still loved me, even though they weren't present. And what is it that the heart is really looking for? Isn't it looking for love and relationship? Right then I encountered the very thing that I wasn't aware of. And I'm still living it now, it doesn't end. It just happens that now I'm here with you. Wide open. Not afraid to tell you anything about myself. I have problems just as bad as the problems I had before. But why am I different now? Why am I able to stand in front of the same problems that I had before, yet not do one single drug? To be honest with you, when I first met my wife, she told me about Fr. Giussani and showed me his book: I opened it up and was like, *What?! You gotta be a Harvard grad to read this book*. But you know what? All of those words and stuff that I thought I couldn't understand? I started to experience them. And when I started to experience them, they became real. I realized I was a person. I realized that I wasn't the one who controlled anything. The most control I could show is depending. I found strength in depending on something greater than myself, which allowed me to see the meaning of my life and its contrasts, to this day.

I'm able to sit here and say, "Yes!" It is the time of the person. I am a person, and these are my people. I'm proud of that. And no, I don't have the answer to why all of these things happened in my life—but I know they happened, and I want more. It's not enough. That little encounter, it didn't quench the thirst of my heart. I want more. And that's why I'm here, to share this message with you. We do this together. This encounter is for all people. It's for *all* people. I'm in love with everyone. But first I had to fall in love with myself and value my life.

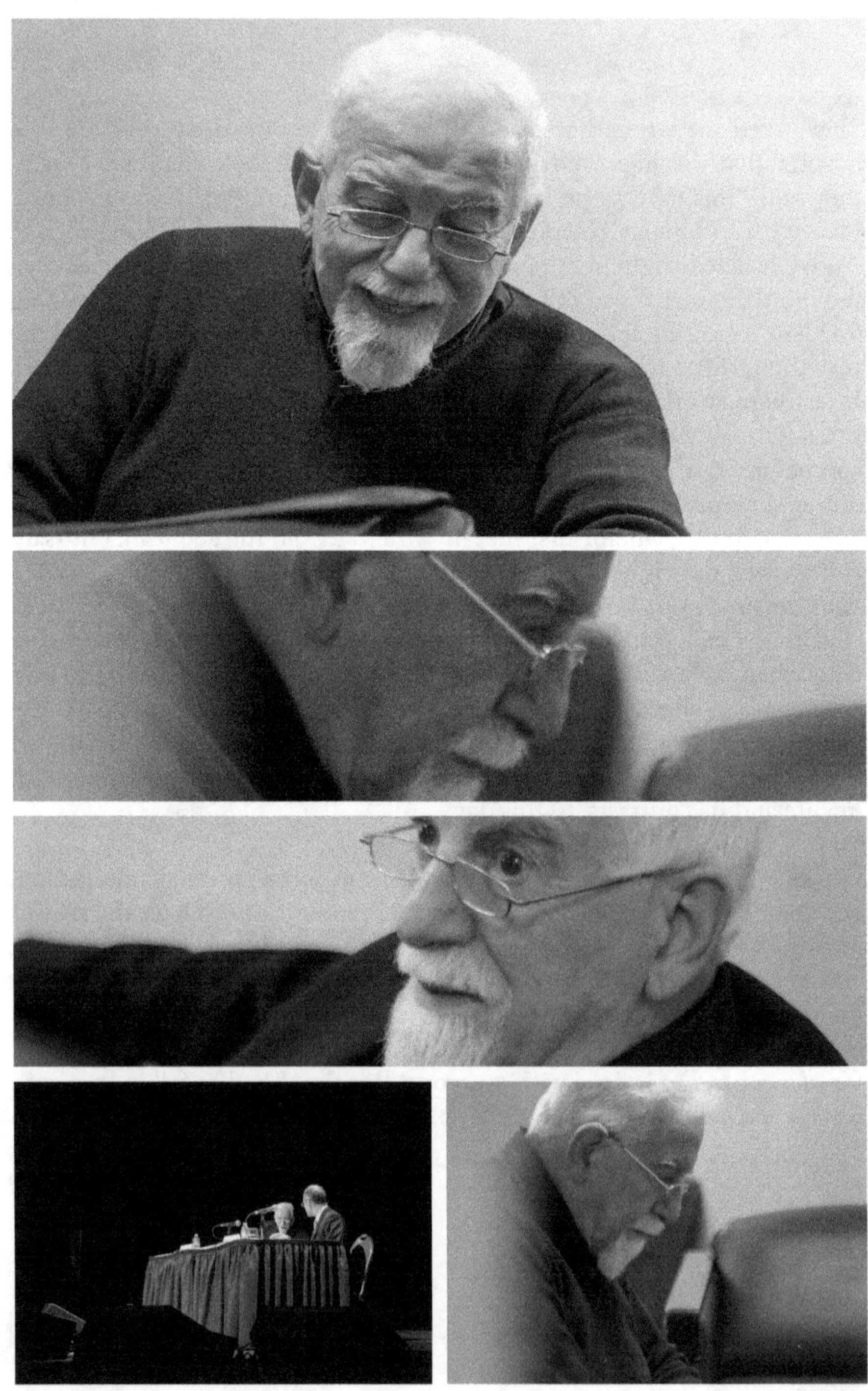

Hoping Against Hope

Fr. Samir Khalil Samir[1]

Introduction

What is the condition of life faced by Christians in many parts of the Middle East? Is it possible to profess and live the Christian faith freely in prevalently Muslim countries? Are there examples in which hatred and divisions have been overcome in the name of the pursuit of a common good rooted in beauty, truth and love?

"Great concern arises from the condition of life faced by Christians who in many parts of the Middle East suffer gravely as a consequence of the current tensions and conflicts underway. Tears still flow in Syria, Iraq, Egypt, and other areas of the Holy Land. The Bishop of Rome will not rest while there are still men and women of any religion, whose dignity is wounded and who are deprived of their basic needs for survival, robbed of their future, or forced to live as fugitives and refugees. Today, we join the Pastors of the Oriental Churches, in appealing that the right of everyone to a dignified life and to freely profess one's own faith be respected. We must not resign ourselves to thinking of a Middle East without Christians, who for 2,000 years have confessed the name of Jesus, and have been fully integrated as citizens into the social, cultural and religious life of the nations to which they belong."

(From the Address of Pope Francis to the Participants in the Plenary Assembly of the Congregation for the Oriental Churches, November 21, 2013)

Saturday, January 18, 2014

[1]Professor of Islamic Studies, University of Saint Joseph, Beirut

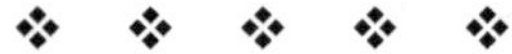

Moderator: How appropriate it is that Father Samir is speaking three days after the Holy Father spoke to pilgrims—including Arab Christians—in Saint Peter's Square, expressing his solidarity with all the persecuted of that region and asking the Arab Christians to always give reasons for their hope. Since on the New York Encounter website you can read a more detailed biography of Father Samir and the litany of his works and accomplishments, I'd like to just point out several aspects of Father Samir's work that have moved me over the years.

First, he's a great scholar. He teaches Islamic studies at the Saint Joseph University in Beirut. It was his rediscovery of medieval Arabic Christian texts, many by theologians and writers forgotten by Western Christianity; and his passionate, tireless effort to research, edit, catalog, and make accessible these texts—that really changed the way that the West and East, including Arab Christians themselves, look at their heritage. In fact, in the 1970s he established in Beirut the Center for Documentation and Research in Arab Christianity, which has continued this work and shared it with other scholars. His books are many, but one I would suggest as a must-read is *111 Questions on Islam*, a volume I refer to often.

Second, Father Samir is a teacher and a mentor. He has taught Christians *and* Muslims. Hundreds upon hundreds of his students have risen to prominent positions in their society and culture, including, I learned yesterday, several current patriarchs in the Arab Church, who wrote their dissertations under him. The story that he told yesterday, of his incredible, historical encounter with Shia leaders in Iraq and Iran, originated through an encounter with a Muslim student who, without converting to Christianity, asked Father Samir to become his spiritual father.

Third, Father Samir is a pastor. For many years now, he travels every summer to Germany and serves in various parishes there.

Fourth, Father Samir is a trusted adviser to Church leaders at the highest levels. Two examples: in 2010, he was a quiet, behind-the-scenes driving force in the organizing and writing of the preliminary documents of the

Middle East Synod of Bishops, truly a work of historic importance; and in 2012, he delivered to all the bishops the final exhortation for all Middle Eastern Christians.

Finally, Father Samir is an astute and penetrating media commentator, whose debates and discussions with various Muslims on Arab TV, or on Lebanese TV, have influenced many people's positive perceptions. He's even appeared on Hezbollah television. I would commend very strongly his analyses and reports that appear on the very important website Asia-News.it. So with that, let me turn it over to Father Samir.

Samir: This morning I was wondering which title could I give as under-title to "Hope Against Hope," and I thought that maybe it could be "Build Together an Open Society." At the end I will explain why. First, some of my own history in connection with what we will discuss this morning. I was born in 1938, went to a Jesuit school until 1955. At that time we didn't always know who was Muslim and who was Christian. In 1948, something happened: the creation of a state where a state was already present. The state of Israel, created by the Society of Nations, in Palestine, where the Palestinians had been living for thousands and thousands of years. The Palestinians didn't come with Islam; the Palestinians were Jewish, and later many became Christian under the Church Fathers. The Muslims came in 636.

The creation of the State of Israel was a great injustice for the Palestinians. It was done as compensation for another, different injustice done to the Jews mainly in Europe. The Society of Nations—which was, at that time, essentially the Western countries—decided, as a reparation, to give the country of another people to the Jews, who were French, German, Polish, Russian, and so on from different nationalities and countries. This changed not only the history of the Middle East but of the world, because the Arab and Muslim countries felt it was an organized aggression from the West against the Arab Muslims. Muslims don't distinguish between their faith, their culture, and their nationality; they put together Arab, Islam, and politics, like other religions, too. Christianity, to my knowledge, is the only exception where religion and politics are well-distinguished, even if not always *well*-distinguished. In the Gospel they are clearly distingushed from the mouth of Christ Himself: give to God what is of God and to Caesar, the emperor, what is his. This is the biggest change, according to my interpretation, that has occurred in the Middle East.

After that the revolutions started. In 1952, the Egyptian revolution occurred, with Gamal and Muhammad Naguib. In 1956, Gamal Abdel Nasser took power in Egypt. Then, between 1956 and 1958, there were revolutions in Syria and Iraq. These revolutions were supposed to bring power to the people. In 1956, we had a new aggression, this time against Egypt; it was in the Suez Canal, the War of Suez. The reason for this was the nationalization of the Suez Canal. The canal belonged to Egypt, but Egypt did not respect her financial agreement with France and England. On this occasion Israel entered the fray, along with France and England, and we had the war resulting in Egypt's defeat. All this was a shock for Muslims in the Middle East and elsewhere. Then we had a reaction, because the agreement of 1948 and 1949, decided by the United Nations, was not applied: based on that agreement, there should be two nations, one for Palestinians, and one for Israelis. It never happened until now. And this was over 60, almost 70 years ago. This is a great injustice. And who is supporting Israel? Globally, it is the West, which we see as a group: the United States, Canada, Europe, Western Europe. And this was seen as such a defeat: all the Arab countries together could not do anything against a very small country, Israel, which was better organized and supported by others.

In 1972, we had the first terrorist act from Palestinians. It was during the Olympic Games in Munich. Why? Because the Palestinians thought the Arab nations would never help them, the West would never help them, the UN was not thinking about them—so they had to do it themselves. They didn't have an army, so they would voluntarily die for the nation. This was seen in Palestine and the Arab countries as a great offering from these persons, who died to save their nation.

I was in Cairo at that time and witnessed in 1973 the beginning of the strong islamization, the radical islamization, of Egypt. In 1973, I was in Minya, southern Egypt, and saw for the first time girls coming to school wearing veils and so-called Islamic dress. This was the beginning.

Now, second point. Why this reaction? The reaction came for three reasons, the first being political. We had two camps: Israel, with the United States and Europe on one side; and the Soviet Union, the worldwide socialist movement, and all the socialist states of the Arab world on the other. The second reason is a very important new element, the religious element. In Saudi Arabia and in the Arab sub-continent we had a new Muslim strain, Wahhabism, from a certain Abd al-Wahhab. This is actually very old, and goes back to 1780, but it took a new form in the 1970s. Wahhabism has a theory which says, "We have to imitate Muhammad, the so-called prophet, the prophet Muhammad, in everything: his way of dressing, of eating, of having sex, of waging war. Since today we are the weakest in the world, we have to do what Muhammad did and lived in order to become the strongest." The theory is: as long as we applied the Quran and the tradition, the Sunnah, and we applied all the specific obligations of Islam, the so-called Sharia—Islam conquered the whole world.

And it is true that in less than ten years, between 632—the date of the death of Muhammad—and 640 the whole Middle East and Persia were conquered by the Muslims. So, this is a fact. The problem is its interpretation. The interpretation was, and is today, "Because they applied Sharia and the traditions perfectly, they won. So, if we want to be the best in the world, we have to apply it, too." This is the core of Wahhabism, which is the theory of Saudi Arabia, but also of the whole Arab sub-country.

The third reason is a cultural one. It is a reality that the Muslim world was, for a while, between the 10th and 13th centuries, a leading cultural power in the world. In medicine especially, but also in physics, mathematics, in philosophy. They did a lot, but I have to underline something. The Syrian Christians are those who translated all that was then existing in the Greek language, first into Syrian, then into Arabic, and thus transmitted it to the Arabs. When I say Arabs, I mean Christian Arabs, Muslim Arabs, Jewish Arabs. Arab is not a religious concept, it is a cultural one. So, we know that the Arabs were culturally advanced in the Middle East. But today they are the last of the lasts, the worst; they say it daily, not to you, but to themselves, when they are among themselves. And they ask, "What have we produced in the modern world? Any creation? In music, literature, history, in science, in anything? Nothing."

So, the Islamic interpretation was, and is, "We were the worst, we are the worst, because we are not rigorously applying the commandments of God, which are given in the Quran and in the Sunnah, the Sharia." This is what we are suffering from, in the whole Arab and Muslim world.

It started to spread in the Arab world in the 1970s, then moved to the Islamic Asiatic world in the 1980s, then eventually came to Europe at the end of the 1980s—probably to America at that time, too. This is a very strong movement, financed by the republics or the monarchies of Arabia, and supported by the Western countries for economic reasons. It is a deformed, radical Islam. Islam was not what we see now. In my opinion, we have never lived what we are living today.

The Muslims say, "Islam is tolerance," and it is true. It was a tolerant religion. Now, I must say that tolerance is not the ideal. I don't want, as a Christian Egyptian, to be tolerated. I am a citizen, and I want simply to be a citizen, to be considered a citizen, not as a Christian, not as a Jew or a Muslim, or anything else. *Egyptian*. This is what we feel daily.

Is there a solution to this situation of radical Islam? First of all, we must acknowledge that the majority of Muslims are not radical. Many of them are suffering because of the radicalism. Muslims used to repeat, "Islam is the religion of the middle. It's not extreme. Neither too spiritual, like-Christianity, nor too political, like radical Islam." So the solution is to build again a Muslim thought, to rebuild the structure of the Arab mentality.

How can we do it? It's a cultural process. We did it once before: in the 19th century, we had in the Arab world what is always called our Renaissance—*Al-Nahda* in Arabic. Who brought about the *Al-Nahda*? Essentially, it was Christians from what at that time was called, under the Turks, Syria—which means today Lebanon, Syria, Jordan, Palestine. The Renaissance came from these people around the middle of the 19th century. In 1860, Christians in Lebanon and Syria were being persecuted by a group of Muslims, the Druze. Some people emigrated to the Americas—Latin America, North America. Others immigrated to Egypt, which at that moment was an open society under the Khedive Isma'il Pasha. They came with their culture, which was a mixture of Arab, Syrian, and Western culture. It would take a little too long to explain how the Western culture was an important factor in Syria—and especially in Lebanon—during these centuries, but it is a well-known fact.

Since the 17th century, the Christians of this region were very much in contact with Western culture. So they came to Egypt and the Khedive asked them to modernize the country. They did it by modernizing the administration, the army, the organization of the country. They did it also by translating over 1,000 books from the Western languages, mainly French but also English and Italian, into Arabic. They created a newspaper and a new literature. Then they created banks, a new economic system. They brought about the cultural revolution that is, as I said, known as our Renaissance. So if we want to change, to build again the Muslim thought, we have to open it to other cultures, to find a new Islamic mixture, a balanced culture.

The second point—the first being to rebuild Muslim thought—is to build together a new society. And by *together* I mean Muslims *and* Christians. I will mention an example of this from the case of Lebanon. The economies of most Arab countries have been depressed, not only for the past few years but for centuries. We have to change the society, the social dimension of the society, to introduce a liberal vision of politics.

Changing politics is what the Arab countries tried to do three years ago with the so-called Arab Spring. It started in Tunisia, moved to Egypt, to Libya, to Bahrain, to Syria and elsewhere. You'll notice that after the spring we've fallen into a winter, a terrible situation where once again radical Islamic thought is predominant. We have to change it together. *Together* is a very important word. It's not a question for just Muslims, it's a national question, and I am a part of the nation just like the Muslim, like the Jew, like the atheist, like anybody. It's not a religious question, but Islam as religion plays a very important role in this situation. Whatever we do must be done together with Muslims.

In the Arab areas where you have Christians, the best schools are usually Christian schools, and they are attended by a lot of Muslims—30% to 50%. They acknowledge that the Christian schools offer the best education possible in our country. Same thing for the hospitals. A lot of things which are Christian and acknowledged as such are considered good, if not the best. So this is not only for us: a Christian school is for everybody, and the majority are Muslims. Two-thirds of our Jesuit school in Cairo are Muslims. This is not a bad solution, because our aim is to build a new mind to change our country in a positive way. And all that Christians can do, we have to do it together with Muslims. The *caritas* we share is not limited to Christians. *Caritas*, love, cannot be particular.

What was asked during the Arab Spring? Liberty, democracy, equality. Liberty, because everywhere we have a *dictature*, dictators. We see it in Syria, we saw it in Egypt, in Iraq, in Saudi Arabia, and all the Arab countries. It could be a monarchy, it could be a so-called republic, but it's always a *dictature*. The only country where we don't have a *dictature* is Lebanon, because Lebanon is a special case in the Middle East. Lebanon is the only Arab country which is not a Muslim country, because Arab doesn't mean Muslim. In Lebanon, when the republic was created, Christians were a slight majority. Today, Christians are around 38%, maybe 40% but no more, because of emigration to the West and because of a lower birthrate than the Muslims. If the trend continues, in 10 years Christians will make up only 33%, maybe 35% of the population.

But Lebanon has something very special. Lebanon is a democracy balanced between Muslims and Christians. Everything in Lebanon must be 50/50. If you create a Christian university today, you cannot recognize it if you don't create a Muslim university in front of it. The feast: a few days ago we celebrated the nativity of the Prophet. It is a feast unknown in other Muslim countries. Why was it created, and why is it a mandatory holiday on which you cannot officially work? Because the Armenians asked to have their Christmas Day, which is the 6th of January. So, in front of the 6th of January, which was a free day, the government created the nativity of Muhammad. This is but one example.

Even though Christians are a little more than the third of the population, in the Lebanese Parliament you have 64 Christians and 64 Muslims, with the Christians arranged proportionally between Orthodox, Catholics, Protestants, and so on, and the Muslims between Sunnah, Shia, Druze, and others. This makes Lebanon a very special country with very special problems. However, the main trend is, "We are one nation, we have the same rights whatever we are." And they are trying to give the same rights to women as to men, because this is one of our greatest problems. There are two problems with regards to equality: one is men/women, the other is Muslim/non-Muslim. On this point Sharia is absolutely unjust: there is no equality between a Muslim and a non-Muslim, and this has been so from the start. While this may have been understandable in former times, it is no longer understandable in a republic.

We have to rethink Islam, as we have to rethink Christianity. The rethinking of Christianity has been going on a long time, especially since Vatican II and into our days. The rethinking of Islam was started in the 19th century and lasted a hundred years, from 1860 to 1970, but now it is closed, we regress. What do I mean by "rethinking"? Start with the Quran: if you say the Quran was dictated by God to Muhammad, who announced it to people who later wrote what they literally heard, then we have the literal word of God. If you have this vision of the Quran, then you say the Quran is the literal word of God and there cannot be anything better in the world. No Gospel, no Bible—nothing could be so perfect as the words of God Himself, so we have to apply it. Even if people say, "This is impossible!" you have to change. However, I contend that the Quran does not have to change, but our interpretation of the Quran does. The Quran started to be reinterpreted in the 19th century, but then they closed the door, as we say in Arabic. We closed the door of the interpretation, so we need to open again that door.

As a conclusion, our mission as Christian Arabs, as Christians in the Arab world: the first essential thing is to live the Gospel. The Gospel is eternal, it is not about small points—"You have to eat like this, or pray like that"—but instead is a spirit, not a letter. As it's written, the letter kills but the spirit vivifies. We must live the Gospel and testify to love, because God is love. This is the Trinity. When they ask me, "How do you say there are three gods?" "We never said three gods." "Yes, you say: Father, Son..."—and I explain that what we mean is what St. John says in the Gospel: God is love, to love means to give, to give myself means to give birth to the Son and the Spirit. If I start with the Trinity, we will debate until the end of the world.

It's impossible to explain the Trinity to a Muslim, and even for myself it is not easy. But maybe the most difficult thing to do is to forgive the one who killed my father, my son; to forgive from my heart.

This is our mission: to live the Gospel. But this is also your mission: to live the Gospel. There is no other vocation for a Christian than to testify to the Gospel, to the love of God for us. And as God has loved us, we love everybody, whatever he or she is. This is important also for us. For American society to find its religious dimension, to rediscover its spirituality, religiosity, and so on, is important for the Arab world, too. This is your task: to maintain in your social and political decisions the spirit of the Gospel against the secular spirit.

And finally, your mission is sharing with the rest of the world: sharing your culture, sharing your financial possibilities, sharing your vision of the world, sharing your ideals. This is our task, yours and mine. You do it in your society, which was originally Christian but not exclusively so, and which sometimes wanders far away from the Gospel. Muslim society is far from the Gospel way of thinking, so we have to bring the spirit of the Gospel closer in everything. We have a common task, and this is beautiful, we can share it: to live the Gospel, to testify to it, personally and as a community, not only as a personal choice. It starts with something personal, but it must be open to changing society and not just myself. It has to be a social project and a political project. Religion and politics in this sense go together, with the meaning that Benedict XVI clarified when he spoke about positive secularism. There is a spirit, which is from the Gospel, and there is a body, a structure of the society, which is from the society. I hope we can give this testimony. I know this is your aim and it is mine, too. This is the most beautiful mission God could give us: to be witnesses to the Gospel.

Moderator: I'd like to share with you, Father Samir, a dream of mine. That someday—soon I hope—we can look out into the audience here at the New York Encounter, and maybe see some of the Iranian imams you met, or somebody Egyptian, Muslim, that you know, and that we can share our experience.

Samir: I hope so.

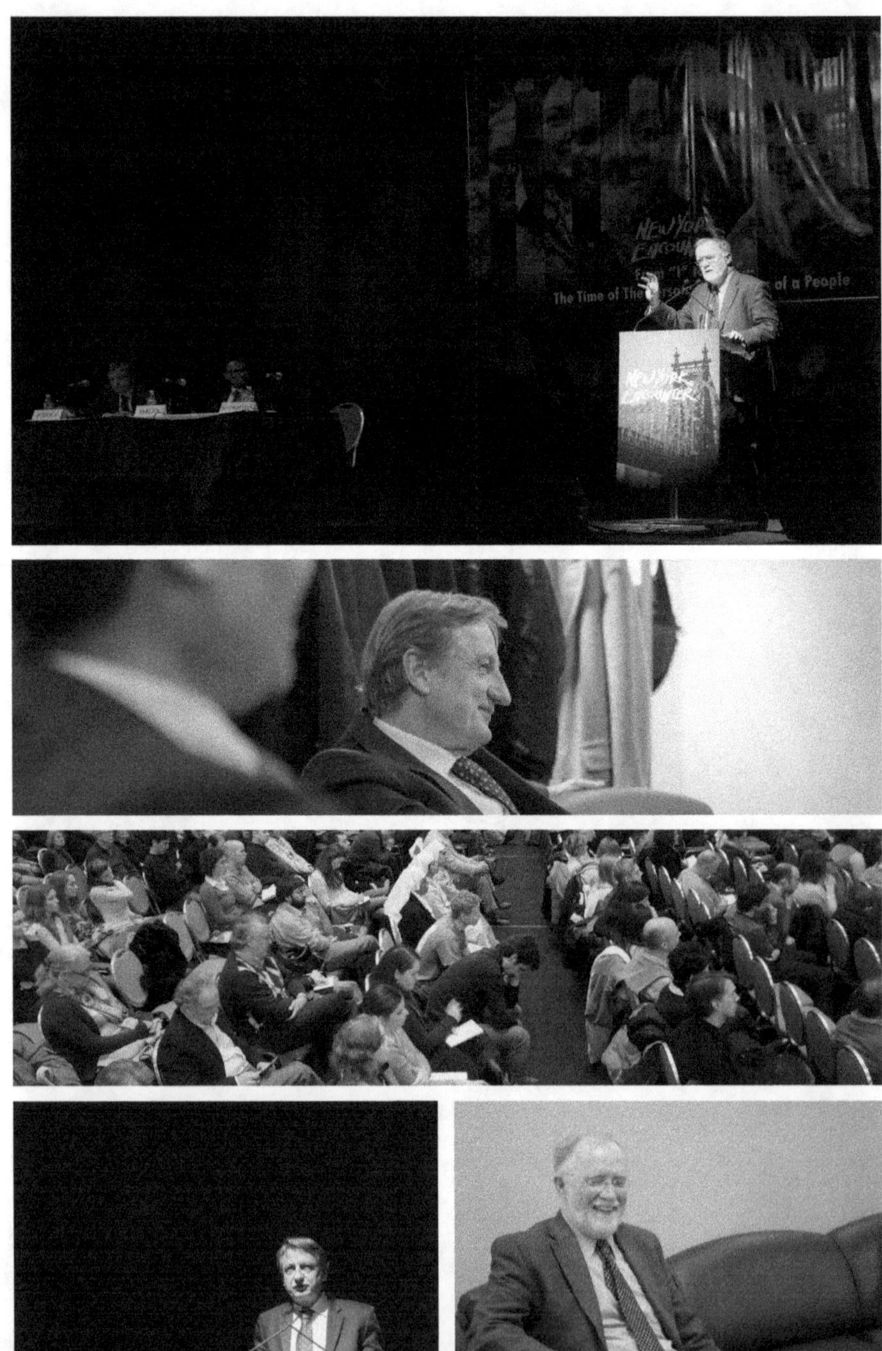
The Time of The
of a People

Is It Possible to Work This Way?

Dr. Michael Naughton[1] and Mr. Bernhard Scholz[2]

Introduction

Is it possible for an entrepreneur to overcome profit maximization as the only criterion giving value to the business endeavor? If so, what is the value of doing business?

What makes a job interesting beyond salary increase or career advancement?

There is a tendency in our culture to think of the economy and work as a fairly impersonal process that can be understood in "scientific" terms and on the basis of an abstract approach. This approach developed, for example, the theory that when acting in the economic sphere, the person is intrinsically egotistical, always behaves in a rational and therefore predictable way, and looks exclusively for profit maximization.

In its turn, this theory led to some misconceptions (which we believe were at the root of the most recent crises): the conviction that the economy must be autonomous and shielded from "influences" of a moral character; the belief that the market, if left alone, creates a balanced system; the exaltation of short-term profit as the main goal of a business; the promotion of an abstract, Darwinian idea of competition and self-reliance; the trust that technology is self-sufficient and does not require a critical and cautious human eye; finally, the confidence that finance can create prosperity even without being related to any value and to real economy. Reality, however, has shown that this abstract approach, especially when human freedom is in play, as it is in economics, does not work and causes large-scale dam-

---

Saturday, January 18, 2014

[1]Director of the John A. Ryan Institute for Catholic Social Thought, University of St. Thomas

[2]President of Compagnia delle Opere (CDO)

age. Economic processes cannot be understood when separated from the people who work and produce. Ultimately, all economic systems reflect the desires, talents, and skills of the people who participate in them. Human beings are not ants, and economic construction is not a mechanical process, but a truly human event that involves reason and freedom at every step. Therefore, is it possible to have a concept of work and business that would mirror the nature of the person, not as self-made and self-sufficient, but as dependent and "in relationship-with"?

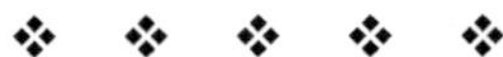

Moderator: This presentation is about exploring whether the purpose of work—the business of business—is truly and exclusively the maximization of profit. And, moreover, that this maximization of profit is determined primarily by the pursuit of corporate and individual self-interest, an approach that thinks about our self interest narrowly and technically. Our human experience in life is certainly much bigger than this. Our lives are much more than what our incomes and salaries alone can measure. Our experience in life is more than just the narrow pursuit of our self-interest—we live in communities with all kinds of relationships that enrich our lives. So, must our experience of work be partial, or can it include all of our humanity, all of our human dynamism? On the other hand, is such a pursuit naive? After all, we live in a highly competitive, globalized world. Running and sustaining a business is hard, and so perhaps businesses should, in fact, maintain a laser focus on maximizing profitability. These other aspects of who we are as human beings are nice and all—one could say—but they are softer factors that do not have a place in the challenging reality faced by businesses everywhere.

Every year, *Fortune* magazine publishes a list of the 100 best companies to work for in the United States. *Fortune* surveys both employees and managers, but they weight the answers of employees by 2/3. They ask the employees three questions: Do they trust the people they work for? Do they have pride in what they do? And do they enjoy the people they work with? These count 2/3 of the overall response. The remaining 1/3 comes from the responses of the managers, who are asked three questions as well: Is the organization achieving its organizational objectives? Do the employees give their personal best? And do people work together as a team/family in an environment of trust? Of these six questions, only one touches on the question of profit. So the Russell Investment Group decided to measure how the stocks of these companies have performed over time. From 1997 to 2013, the overall stock market in the US rose 6% per year. The top 100 best companies to work for saw their stocks rise 12% per year, twice as much as the overall stock market. I thought this was very compelling. I work for an investment company and we are always looking to invest in those companies that will maximize profits. This study suggests that the most successful companies may, in fact, be those companies that take a more holistic view of our humanity. At a minimum, this study suggests that companies that focus on these factors—perceived by some as "soft"—are not necessarily companies that will be less profitable.

To help us better approach the question of how we can engage work with all of our humanity, we have today two terrific speakers.

Naughton: On this topic—"Is it Possible to Work This Way?"—I'd like to mention a document that has come out from the Pontifical Council for Justice and Peace, called "The Vocation of the Business Leader," which is up on your screens right now. It's in 16 languages at the current time. I do hope, whether you are a business person, a teacher, doctor, truck driver, nurse, plumber, or whatever you might be, that you will find some value in this document, because it talks about the nature of work. And whether you are religious or not, I also hope the document can speak to your fundamental sense of humanity.

The subtitle of this talk—"Confronting the Logic of the Market with the Logic of the Gift"—offers two different ways of looking at the question of work. To help us get at this theme, which I've been hearing throughout the conference, talking to people particularly in CL—it has to be connected to the stories of our lives. For many of us sitting in this room—actually all of us sitting in this room—we have an understanding of work, but sometimes we are not always conscious of what it is, and it's important that the ideas that I will talk about today be connected to the ideas of your stories. What are the stories of your life?

Is it Possible to Work This Way?

I grew up on the South Side of Chicago to Irish immigrant parents. I was sixteen when, one day, I walked out the door and my father looked at me and said, "Michael…Michael, you be a good boy." I said, "Sure, Dad, whatever." And before I could take another step, my father looked at me and said, "Michael, and if you can't be good…you be careful." I said, "Alright. I think I can do that." Well, an unfortunate event happened to me that night, and my father had to pick me up from a Chicago police station. I'll spare you the details about why he had to do that. But he walked into the police station, he looked at me and he said, "Michael…Michael, I think you'd better just be good."

Now, we live in a culture that is constantly talking about the idea of being careful. We have designated drivers—safe and careful drivers who take home drunk and stupid friends. We have this thing called safe sex, somehow thinking that non-productive, disease-free sex will make up for its procreative and unitive meaning. We have a school system that is constantly concerned about test scores and grades, yet our students have lost the love of learning. We find ourselves in our own career strategies, trying to figure out how we can get to the next step, yet we have lost the sense of what good work is. All this talk about being careful loses sight and distracts us from this fundamental sense about what it means to be good at our work, and this is exactly what this document is about, the vocation of the business leader: it's about being good, as well as about being careful and being intelligent. It's about being good, not in some superficial or extrinsic sense, not in terms of a series of slogans that can sometimes be found, particularly in business—in terms of having integrity, in terms of having corporate social responsibility, in terms of having business ethics, right? All of those things can sometimes find themselves turning into slogans.

We had a presentation this morning, a wonderful presentation about Vaclav Havel, who had, in a sense, a similar concern, particularly about the nature of human rights. He said this: "Politicians may reiterate a thousand times that the basis of the new world order must be universal respect for human rights, but it will mean nothing as long as this imperative does not derive from respect for the miracle of the universe, for the miracle of nature, the miracle of our own existence." Havel was concerned that "human rights" was becoming a slogan. That it was, in a sense, becoming something like cut flowers: it looked pretty, everyone seemed to enjoy it, but by its very nature it was atrophying, it was decaying, because fundamentally it had lost a deep sense of a root system. If our ethic fails to be grounded in something that's more than simply law, something that's more than simply a platitude, something that's more than a generic value commitment, our ethic will grow cold, and in a while it will have lost its ability to do what it's supposed to do. What we need, then, is a deep root system. We need a deep logic.

This document, along with what the social tradition, particularly the Catholic social tradition, speaks about, is a logic of gift, and it's exactly what is at the heart of this document, a logic of gift. The document starts off with a quote from Jesus in the Gospels, where Jesus says: "From everyone who has been given much, much will be demanded, and from the one who has been entrusted with much, much will be asked." The logic here is a logic that we have received, that we have been gifted, which we in turn are to give. That is the nature of one's vocation: receiving and giving. I'll come back to this point a little bit later in the talk.

This logic of the gift, however, is very different than simply the logic of the market *only*. I emphasize *only*. Whereas the logic of the gift presupposes that something is given, the logic of the market presupposes that nothing is given and is only acquired. You have to assail nature and grab things out of it, and then it becomes yours. Whereas the logic of the gift presupposes that we are chosen, the logic of the market sees only discreet individual choices, one being no better than the other; we are simply the arbitrators of our own choices.

To get at this question of choices, and chosen-ness, there's a wonderful book by a Jewish sociologist, Philip Rieff, called *The Triumph of the Therapeutic*. This is what Rieff said: "There is no feeling more desperate than that of being free to choose and yet without the specific compulsion of being chosen." The logic of the market often says that choice is the highest value—not the content of the choice—yet we know that choice by itself does not have the capacity to give meaning to our work. Rieff goes on to say: "After all, one does not really choose, one is chosen." This is one way of stating the difference between gods and men. Gods choose, men are chosen. The deepest sense of the human spirit is this deep sense that we are called, that life often distracts us from the call, and we too often forget what the call is. Finally, Rieff says: "What men lose when they become as free as gods is precisely that sense of being chosen which encourages them in their gratitude. To take their subsequent choices seriously." We cannot separate being free to choose and being chosen, and when we break this, we often take our choices less seriously.

The wonderful literary writer D.H. Lawrence put it this way: "Men are not free when they are doing just what they like—the moment you can do just what you like there's nothing you care about doing. Men are free when they are obeying some deep inward voice of religious belief." Too often, our choices can create a small world. St. Augustine in *The Confessions* says: "The house of my soul is too small for you to come to it; may it be enlarged by you."

Can we work this way? Can we work with this idea, of this deep sense of being chosen? This document says Yes, and it provides some specific forms. The document is structured in a See, Judge, Act method, and it says this: "An important part of one's vocation entails seeing clearly the situation, judging with principles that foster the integral development of people, and acting in a way which implements these principles in light of one's circumstances." If we are to work as a vocation, we have to have a structure of how we see and judge and act in reality. This is what Thomas Aquinas called "practical wisdom"—how to be wise in practical affairs. And so the document tries to describe what this practical wisdom looks at. So let's look at each one—Seeing, Judging and Acting.

Seeing. What does the leader see? Or what do you see when you go to work? Key to this is sensitizing yourself to what you see, and this—the seeing—is about seeing things whole and not just partly: seeing the whole of reality and not merely a part of reality.

There is a very famous philosopher in this country by the name of Alasdair McIntyre. He has argued that universities are increasingly losing their capacity to help their students see things whole—to see, in a sense, how things are in relationship with each other—because they have become so specialized that they've lost sight of the whole. McIntyre says that our current economic recession, the Iraq War, the Middle East, the growing economic inequality, the Iranian revolution back in the '70s—were all products of misjudgments by a highly intellectual elite, highly educated people. The problem with them was not that they didn't have more specialized training; the problem, according to McIntyre, is that they had lost the habit of mind of seeing things *whole*.

Seeing is also about seeing fact and value, not just numbers. Any of you who are in organizations will also know the slogan: "If it cannot be measured, it does not exist." But this spirit is exactly what prevents us from seeing reality. It distorts the vision that we often bring to what we do at work. And the seeing is also about seeing beyond neighbors, to fraternity, to seeing people not just simply as entities, but as brothers and sisters. A friend of mine who runs a construction company in Mexico City once said to me, "When I encounter a lot of American CEOs, they often speak about their employees as employees, but they often don't see that these are family members. They are mothers and fathers and brothers and sisters." Thus how we see is of critical importance. We often see in our workspaces permanent whitewater rapids—things are changing fast and it's hard to get a firm grasp on what's being seen.

In the document, it speaks about four things business people see: globalization; communication technology; financialization of the economy; and cultural changes. All of these bring a great deal of complexity to the business world, and make it difficult sometimes to know how to act. But all of them, in many respects, beg the question: "What principles do you use to make judgments?"

Judging. And so we come to the second aspect of the structure of this document: judging with principles, because in order to see well, we have to be able to judge well. The two are intrinsically bound together, so judging is about being formed in first principles that can guide decisions that foster the integral development of people. The document says: "The ability to reason, to make reasoned judgments, must be nurtured in the moral and spiritual culture from which business leaders come, namely their families, religion, educational institutions, and the larger communities to which they belong. Neither business nor government can produce its own moral capital. What produces the moral capital is out of the culture from which people come. So key to judgment is the family, is the church, is education."

But these principles do something else—they remind us and they reveal for us the purpose of the trip, because one of the biggest problems for all of us sitting in this room is amnesia. We often forget the good. We sometimes forget the purpose of the trip. These principles also, in a sense, help us locate the good that business should do. Every institution should articulate a set of goods that define what they do, and this document identifies three goods of business: 1) good goods; 2) good work; and 3) good wealth.

Business is about good goods. It's about making goods that are truly good, and offering services that truly serve. Often, many of us think we don't have a vocation because we don't think what we do is very big. But this is how we get access to the goods of the world, in business or whatever discipline we enter. It's how we get food and shelter and transportation and clothing and energy. This is a very good thing. It is ordinary in the best sense of the word—the sense the Church uses in speaking of Ordinary Time. What we do in the ordinary way can also be a very good thing. The problem, however, is that the logic of the market often reduces this ordinariness to either legality or price, and this is often the thing they describe as good.

The second good is good work. Business is about organizing work where employees develop their gifts and talents, that help them exercise their talents and their abilities in what they do.

In 1931, Pope Pius XI wrote an encyclical called *Quadragesimo Anno*, in which he says this: "Why is it that matter goes into factories and comes out noble products, yet workers go into factories and come out degraded." We have to be concerned about good work in all the institutions that we have.

And thirdly, good wealth: creating sustainable wealth and distributing it justly. You cannot distribute what you have not created; but neither can you create wealth without addressing how you distribute it. These three goods help us to resist the temptation we spoke about at the beginning of this session: to reduce business to a unidimensional reality, to simply profit—the so-called bottom line of business. But here's the interesting thing. This temptation is common to all institutions. We are seeing it today in marriage—reducing marriage to simply one good, the sentiment of the couple. Reducing education to simply a credential and a career. Our institutions need a robust sense of goods, and for all of us who find ourselves in those institutions, our vocation is, in a sense, to build up those goods, to make them good institutions.

So what ought we do? The third part: *acting*. Interestingly enough, *The Vocation of the Business Leader* does not start off with a list of things to do, but rather with this first act. The first act within the logic of gift is to receive what God has done for us, to receive the Scriptures, to honor the Sabbath, to pray, to participate in the deep silence of human life. That provides the receptivity to provide a deep well of reflection about how to see the reality of the world. The Sabbath, for example, is not an escape from work, but rather it detaches us from work to help us see work more clearly. The key thing is this idea of receptivity.

The second act the document talks about is the act of giving. The second act is to give in a way that responds to what we have received. Mr. Scholz will be up here pretty soon, speaking about what one should be doing, about good work, about good goods, and about good wealth; I'll leave that to him. These two actions are of critical importance, in a rhythm. Later today you'll be hearing from, I think, one of the best and most creative theologians in America, David Schindler, who provides a wonderful synthesis of these two actions. He says: "When we first experience our being as created, as being gifted life, this receiving enables us to see our doing and having as ways of giving, which they were meant to be." It's a powerful statement. I think what David Schindler is talking about, and this is exactly what *The Vocation of the Business Leader* is talking about, is that if we don't get receptivity right, we'll never get giving right. If we don't get rest right, or leisure right, or prayer right, we'll never get work right. If we don't get the Sabbath right, we'll never get Monday right.

Benedict XVI has a wonderful line where he says: "The person comes to the profoundest sense of himself not through what he does, but through what he accepts. Not through what he achieves, but through what he receives." This is probably the hardest thing for a business person to get, that the key thing in their lives is not what they achieve; instead, the key thing is to recognize what they have received.

So: is it possible to work this way? Actually, this is the only way to work, because it is built into our DNA to receive and give—the rhythm of receptivity and of giving.

Let me conclude with the final quote, which I thinks sums up the heart of what this document is about. It comes from John Henry Newman, who said this: "God created me to do Him some definite service. He has committed some work to me, which He has not committed to another. I have my mission. I never may know it fully in this life, but I shall be told it in the next. Somehow I am necessary to His purposes. I'm a link in a chain; a bond of connection between persons. He has not created me for naught."

Scholz: Thank you for this invitation, which is for me an opportunity to reflect more deeply upon the origins and the perspectives related to our work and to our businesses.

1) Introduction: fundamental questions

The association CDO was born in 1986 by a provocation of Father Giussani, who asked some of the friends of Communion and Liberation why their friendship didn't involve the real needs of people. He then invited them to "help everything exist."

Since its beginning, CDO was engaged with the meaning of work and entrepreneurship in both the for-profit and non-profit worlds. In the last few years, questions have grown and intensified because of the financial and economic crisis that we are experiencing.

As a matter of fact, this crisis is not just a cyclical problem, it is the end of an epoch that we can outline with clarity, and the beginning of a new one that is still to be constructed. I will try to summarize this transformation, considering three aspects.

The first aspect. With the entry of new countries into the international market, so-called globalization, and with the end of the economic prevalence of North America and Europe, there have been direct or indirect consequences for all companies and professionals of the world. We need new business strategies and new political rules allowing a fair exchange of goods and services—without privileges and without monopolies—for all countries.

The second aspect. In the relationship between finance and economics, we can see that finance being an end in itself, and finance as exploitation of the real economy, is no longer sustainable. Finance is necessary and indispensable to the economy, but it is not an aim in itself. Economy must be at the service of the common good, and finance should serve economy.

The third aspect. We must look at the role of the State in economic development. Too often, especially in Europe, the governments were called to save everything. This has often reduced the sense of personal responsibility and solidarity, and boosted a public debt that will penalize future generations. The State must make rules to create the conditions for a correct economy and take action to help those in need, those who can't find a real support. But first of all its task is to open spaces and sustain in the logic of subsidiarity all the educational, social, cultural, and economic initiatives of civil society—using the most appropriate ways related to the culture of each people.

Most people understand these challenges, knowing well that there are no automatic answers and that there are no new models ready to be applied. We are in a period of deep transformation, the aim of which is to create a new future, in the direction of a more human society with a sustainable economy.

At this point, a fundamental question arises for each of us: are we just spectators or even passive victims of this transformation, or can we intervene actively and contribute positively to this evolution?

The answer is *Yes.*

We can do it starting from our working and entrepreneurial experience, capturing its educational and cultural values. If we look carefully at the three macro factors that I have listed, we can see that they all have their roots in a series of anthropological problems. What is the meaning of work? What is the meaning of being a company? What is the meaning of economy? What is the responsibility of each individual and of the associations within the civil society? How can the States realize their responsibility?

If we do not find true and meaningful answers to these questions, it is unlikely that this transformation will be successful. The first and most important contribution each of us can make in this phase is the rediscovery of the meaning of work and of the way of doing business—together with an open dialogue between society and politics.

2) The meaning of our work and personal growth

I would like to comment, in this regard, on some experiences related to the nature and dynamics of our work.

We have in our association some professional training schools dedicated to boys and girls coming from disadvantaged social and family situations. These trainings alternate between work experience and school, getting the young people to know, on the one hand, how to become cooks, hairdressers, mechanics, carpenters, accountants, etc.; and, on the other hand, teaching them literature, mathematics, history, and often a foreign language.

The amazing thing is the result. After attending these schools, boys and girls at the age of about 18 are really competent, talented, interested, and motivated. The work experience and the professional knowledge are for them an opportunity to express their talents and interests. They gain an in-depth knowledge of a particular activity and live a positive relationship with others—none of which is taken for granted by them; it is a true and dynamic discovery. They become proud of their work, and in addition they learn something else not to be taken for granted: the sense of responsibility.

Many of these girls and guys take internships in different companies. Entrepreneurs who allow them to work in their companies do not receive any kind of economic return. They do it with a true enthusiasm demonstrated, for example, by the great patience shown in picking the young people up from home in the morning, when they do not want to get up! And the entrepreneurs themselves are often surprised to understand that for these young people work is the first big chance to have an experience of self-discovery, and this experience can also be useful for those who accompany them in life and work.

The Italian CEO of an international chain of hotels relates how this experience of working with our professional school has impacted him: "We have pushed hard to have young people do internships with us, in order to give them the opportunity to understand what real life is. But...the most important aspect was to be able to bring together these young people who had difficult life experiences and have them work with people who probably enjoyed easier journeys. So all this becomes a form of help for all of us, giving us the chance to re-evaluate our own priorities in life."

An electrician who has taken on one of these guys says: "Honestly, it is not a risk, but it is my desire and my privilege to explain to young people the job to be done, and relate it to the working environment."

If we really want a more human society and economy, we cannot fail to share the meaning of work that is reflected in these statements and in the experience of these young persons.

I would like to highlight some aspects that have emerged with greater clarity:

The first aspect is the most immediate: a job allows one to live, to create a family, to get to know the world.

The second aspect concerns self-knowledge: when I am in action, I can get to know myself, my talents and my virtues, helping me not to be discouraged by my limits. I understand that a job can make me grow not only professionally but also as a human being.

The third aspect concerns relationships. Normally, the job is a chance to develop relationships with other people. These relationships are as difficult as they are desired. This is due to the fact that it is impossible to live and to become ourselves without relationships, although these very relationships are deeply challenging. They help me to discover, often through a lot of difficulties, the true value of myself and of others.

The fourth aspect concerns the satisfaction coming from the experience of being useful, of being able to do something that is useful for others, regardless of one's position in the company (if there was no one to clean the room we are in now, our meeting wouldn't have been possible). Everyone can make an important contribution to transforming reality into a more human environment, and, directly or indirectly, put it at the service of our true needs.

Our work is first and foremost an expression of our life, of our desire to live in a better way and to live with others, of our desire to express ourselves and our talents and, not least, of our desire to be useful to the world around us.

There is a big difference between suffering work only as something you have to do, and facing it as a privileged opportunity to become yourself and to grow even in difficult conditions. Those who come from difficult life conditions paradoxically often understand life better than others. This kind of person doesn't take anything for granted, and searching for a full meaning makes it a more profound and lasting experience. So much so that the young people of our training schools are often hired before other young people, because they have a higher and stronger motivation.

The real problem today seems to be more and more the reduction of work to a merely instrumental factor of individual enrichment or individual power. These individualistic reductions are one of the anthropological reasons leading to the manipulation of all human activities: it leads to the short-term profit ideology and to the use of power as a means to gratify oneself without considering the good of others. But facing work in this limited way will never bring true satisfaction, and this is the reason why the fixation on money and career becomes more and more fierce and violent. People who grow accustomed to this mind-set become, sooner or later, depressed, and live with a resentment that isolates them more and more.

So how is it possible to overcome these reductions, this idolatry of work? For the answer let's go back to the girls and guys of our vocational schools. How did they get out of their situation, a situation they faced with resignation, often without hope? They did it because they met someone who believed in them, someone who valued them, someone who showed a free interest in them, someone who communicated to them that their lives have an infinite value. These young people began to understand that within themselves they had an infinite desire waiting to be released and to become a force enabling them to experience true life—bringing about a change in their very selves and in their relationship with the world around them.

Every one of us is infinitely more than what we can do. What we do helps us to *understand* who we are, but it doesn't ever *define* who we are. We are not defined by the circumstances of our life, or by our successes or our failures. But how we deal with the circumstances, how we work is the expression of what we really believe, of what we really trust in: work is an expression of our self-consciousness. Work gives us the possibility of knowing ourselves more and more and of becoming more and more what we are meant to be.

If we are not aware of who we are, then we will try to increase the value of our life through what we do—namely, by means of the appearances that we will create around ourselves. Without a truly free encounter that opens us to the experience of ourselves, our work tends to be a continuous assertion of ourselves. On the other hand, if a person has the experience of being fully accepted in an unconditional way, then his work becomes what it really is: a service able to give a large contribution to the realization of the self and to the realization of the world. In this way our work becomes a way to educate ourselves, and this is true not only for young people but also for adults. It is an education to a creative and responsible form of freedom.

3) The meaning of doing business and the willingness to change

The second experience I want to share relates to the meaning of enterprise, the sense of a company. For almost ten years now, our association has been organizing something we call "Matching." This is an international meeting between businesses of all sectors of production and services, whereby entrepreneurs and managers meet and share information, knowledge, and experience useful for business development. Along with a lot of individual meetings, there are a large number of workshops with presentations of new markets in other countries, with examples of new ways to manage business and collaborations between different companies.

The novelty of Matching—in which more than 2,000 small and medium-sized enterprises participate—attracted the interest of a researcher from a British university who organized a three-year case study. One of the results of this research was to show that those who benefited most from Matching were those who conceived of it as a kind of training for themselves, carried out through dialogue with others. This dialogue drew out personal potential and possibilities for change that, in the daily internal communication activity of a company, would never have emerged with such clarity and such strength. One manager said: "Matching has been very important for me in terms of openness and growth of knowledge...I understood that before doing some things we need a better comprehension and must think about them...The solution is not necessarily working more but working better." And an entrepreneur pointed out: "Matching's usefulness is not only measurable in terms of business brought home; it's first of all a great entrepreneurial school...a balancing of our entrepreneurial propensities with others who live the same problems. Matching offers a sort of exercise in comparing with other entrepreneurs in a direct way, without barriers."

When people speak of the aim of an enterprise, normally they put profit at the center. But the dialogues that take place during Matching bring out clearly that the purpose of business is not profit but "creation of customers," to use a successful expression of Peter Drucker. Of course, profit is an absolute necessity in developing any company, but it is not the purpose. All the positive tension of these business owners and managers, who talk to each other with sincerity and interest, is based on the fact that they conceive their businesses as a collaboration between individuals who, to obtain the satisfaction of current and future clients, must succeed in a consistent and long-lasting way in the market. Profit is a necessary consequence of this approach, and only this approach opens to a long-term perspective and a higher probability of creating employment. It is for this reason that they are aware of the need for continuous change, and are willing to innovate even when it is challenging. If the main interest of a company was the shareholder value or a short-term profit goal, there would be far less interest in real development, and there would not be this climate of trust and openness that characterizes Matching.

During Matching we can see the evolution of the idea of competition as something really useful for everyone. In the common business mentality, the concept of competitiveness tends to be fierce and warlike. But the market can be seen as a war of *mors tua vita mea*—death for you, life for me—which often happens. Or instead it can be faced as a useful and provocative comparison which invites all players to develop the best of what they are able to do. The purpose of the market is not to eliminate others but—together with the value of choice—to provoke the best in everyone.

By means of Matching, many companies started working together and created networks that generated synergies between their different skills, knowledge, and expertise. This overcoming of the mistrust of others, and, at the same time, increasing the success of businesses working together for common growth, often extends to cooperating with companies of other countries. In this way, we are positively and constructively addressing globalization.

When a company really follows its original nature and allows people to work well, it becomes useful for everyone: for those who work there, for those who benefit from its products and services, and also for society, which grows with the creation of jobs and the empowerment of people. All this calls for a management based on shared responsibility and a seamless sharing of objectives and instruments, allowing the involvement of all.

4) Conclusions

Let me conclude with a final thought. It has become evident that the real change needed to transform our society and our economies is in the self-consciousness we have and the experience of work we live. As it turns out, this is not a set of morals or ethics, but the discovery of the nature of our person and our work, the nature of a company and economy. Either our work is considered an expression of an open, creative, and supportive personal identity, or it becomes self-assertion with an impossible and ultimately violent claim to create one's own identity through success. Either our companies are working places serving our customers and the users, or they are places where we have a short-term gain and consequently a long-term distortion of business and economy. It is not a moral question but a matter of fact that it is not possible to achieve, in the long term, a good for myself or my company if I don't consider the good of the others who stay in relationship with me.

You can understand, then, that the Christian experience is a very decisive factor in a real transformation of the economy. It starts from new players, and is able to discover or rediscover with the intelligence of faith the original dynamics of work—beginning with the person himself. Thus one arrives at the meaning of solidarity in economy. It is in this regard that the Church's social doctrine is extremely useful as a fundamental orientation. But the map doesn't substitute for the journey; good advice cannot take away the risk of the adventure.

Living the true meaning of work is not possible through the application of a theory, but only through a personal experience. When this experience doesn't exist, people take refuge in rules and in the dissemination of ethical advice. This has never generated free and responsible people who live their work as an expression of themselves and of their authentic desire to create a better world for all. The world does not change for the better by "applying" precepts; it changes only by "generating" something new while remaining faithfully connected to the desire for beauty and truth inscribed in the heart of each person.

The time taken for the journey of transformation is not in our hands. Each of us has the task of starting by taking the first steps. And because whether these steps are going in the right direction depends on each of us, it makes a lot of sense to go together within a great company, sustaining everyone in his own personal responsibility. Christian experience can therefore become the leaven for a new development in which the good of persons, the good of our work and the good of civil society, become meaningfully and creatively related.

Moderator: Is it possible to work this way? That was the title of this session. It is a question that seeks to understand if all of our humanity is engaged in work, or whether we are forever relegated to living partial lives in the work place. I think both of our speakers offered some very compelling insights and experiences on how we can engage in work anew.

Professor Naughton focused on the document, *The Vocation of the Business Leader*, and I would really encourage you all to read and work on this document. It is really a tremendous piece that offers a great starting point for anyone working, as it addresses our grave tendency to live divided lives. It is very readable and very practical, as it does not ignore the realities that businesses face in today's world.

Mr. Scholz highlighted three particular economic challenges of our time —the globalization of businesses, the misuse of finance in its relationship with the economy, and the changing role of the state in addressing our economic challenges. He asked an important question: whether we, each one of us here, can intervene and respond to these challenges. Mr. Scholz's response was an emphatic *Yes*. These challenges are not primarily problems of power; these are problems of culture, how each one of us thinks about the meaning of work. Mr. Scholz offered us two distinct experiences that showed that companies can, in fact, embrace the human condition more fully, not as something added on top of the business, but as facets that emerge from the same source that desires to build and grow a business. The human "I" remains unified.

Personally, I really enjoyed preparing for this event, and find myself provoked to engage my work and company differently. I would invite you all to take up this challenge, this work, because the change we seek in the workplace can only happen if there is a change in our cultural conception of work. There is no top-down solution to this challenge—we need not wait for our bosses and politicians to start with a new gaze on the meaning and value of our work.

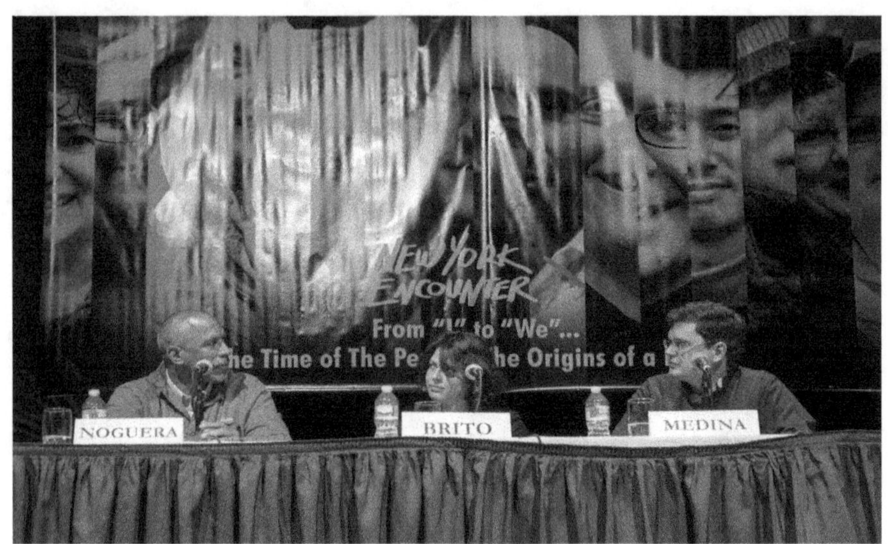
NEW YORK ENCOUNTER
NOGUERA
BRITO
MEDINA

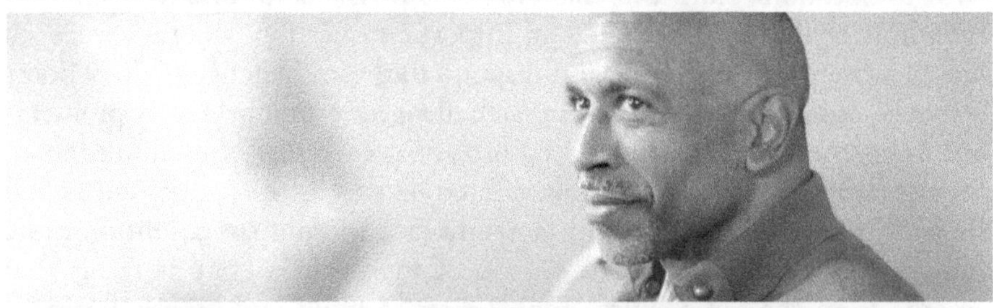

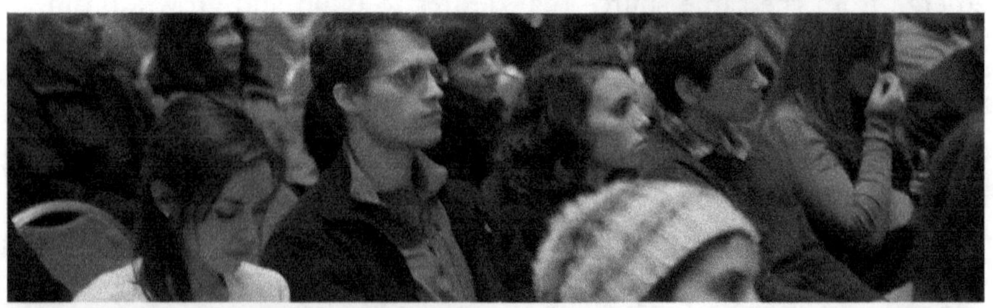

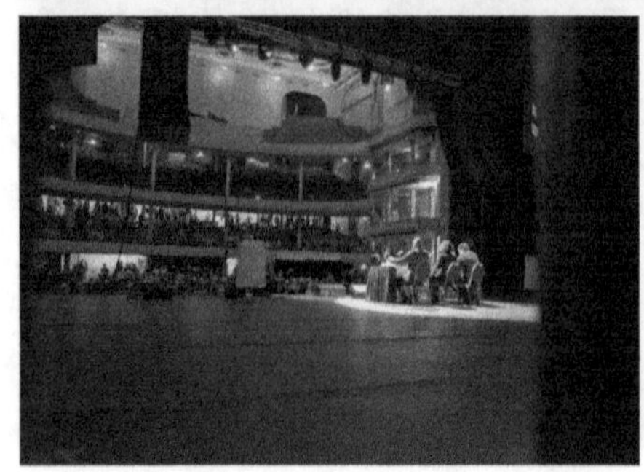

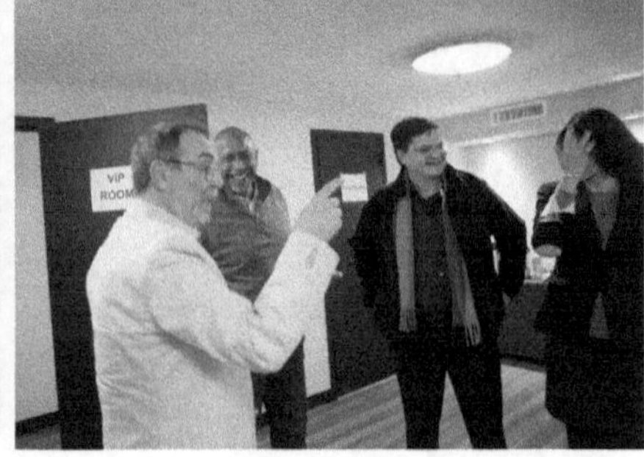

Lost?

Fr. José Medina[1] and Dr. Pedro Noguera[2]

Introduction

It is undeniable that the "tyranny" of fashion, the feeling of being estranged from oneself, the atrophy of desire, are common threads among young generations. There is also a sense that juvenile violence, from bullying to the extreme of school shooting, is escalating. What are the roots of this often-blind violence? What might these recurring acts of violence reveal about human nature? What role can education play as a response to the current situation?

Already in 1987, Msgr. Luigi Giussani was speaking about youth alienation in these terms:

"I observe a difference between the current generation of youth and the one I met thirty years ago. The difference lies in a weakness in the realm of awareness, a weakness that is not ethical, but concerns the dynamism of the awareness. [...] It is as if the youth of today were victims of a kind of Chernobyl nuclear explosion: their organism remains structurally the same but dynamically it is different. There has been a sort of physiological subjugation operated by a dominant mentality. It is as if the only real evidence in reality is what is in fashion, and fashion is a concept and an instrument of power. Never before has the environment—understood as mental climate and way of life—had at its disposal instruments of such invasive and despotic power over our consciences [...] Our surroundings, the dominant mentality, the all-invasive culture [...] cause us to feel estranged from ourselves. So we remain, on the one hand, abstracted in the relationship with ourselves and emotionally discharged (like batteries that last for minutes

---

Saturday, January 18, 2014

[1]Teacher and U.S. Coordinator of Communion and Liberation
[2]Peter L. Agnew Professor of Education, New York University

instead of hours); and on the other hand, by contrast, we try to find shelter in the community [...] The program of the dominant culture is to reduce the person [...] to suffocate and reduce the desires, almost to atrophy their originating source."

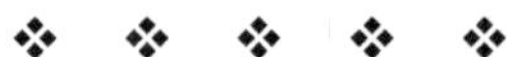

Moderator: Last night we heard a speaker declare on stage, "I used to think that I wasn't a person," as he recalled wanting to jump on a passerby for money. As Frank explained beautifully, a lack of empathy, connection, and overwhelming desperation prefaces acts of aggression in a way that is too familiar in our society and now in our schools.

Teaching at an urban school for the past four years, I have watched students suffocate their personhood through different means. "I don't care," "I don't trust nobody," they would say, or, "I'd rather post my mood on Facebook than talk to you about it," or worse yet, "It's easier to tell that kid what you think of him online than it is to deal with him here." Although these kinds of responses are not unique to low-income communities, I find it significant that kids living in urban violence and poverty have higher levels of institutional distress, more difficulty building connections with adults, and even greater difficulty creating solidarity with each other. These are well-known survival strategies in indifferent environments. More and more we find that the correlation between social isolation and violence mirrors urban context. We have seen it in suburban schools, malls, movie theater shootings, all in a typically white world. So in a world where most adults have developed greater institutional and political distress, the general American public is weak in solidarity groups and cultural fears, individualism. I wonder if we are not creating these indifferent environments everywhere for our children. In this conversation we want to explore the need for education in the wake of both the publicized and anonymous violence, in places like Newtown, Boston, or even Harper High in Chicago.

To begin, we want to open up with a couple of really simple questions. Dr. Noguera and I were just discussing this, and he's previously discussed it with Fr. José. About a year ago, he wrote an article in which he mentioned that we live in a violent society with far too many guns, far too much anger, and way too much alienation. Now this article, I should preface, was written just a few weeks after the Newtown shootings, and he mentions that the real problem is that the social contract is fraying, the bond that should prevent individuals from harming one another has deteriorated. If all we do to seek solutions to the fraying thread of violence is enact and increase security measures, then we continue to ignore the real source of our security: civic solidarity. So we want to discuss some of those ideas.

First of all, as an AP Government teacher, I love the solution you proposed about civic solidarity. It's right up my alley. But to you, what does that look like? And is *trust* another word for civic solidarity? I hear that the last speaker also spoke about trust. So, what is that trust, where is it coming from, and how is it educated?

Noguera: It's a pleasure to be here. I wrote that article because I was very concerned that the first response to the Newtown shooting was to call for armed teachers, police and security guards in schools, continuing down a path of more security—in some cases even creating schools that are much more like prisons than learning centers. And I wanted to remind people that the real source of our safety, the real source of our security, is not in the presence of armed men, but in our relationships. And these relationships—John Locke described this—are a social contract: relationships that are rooted in an understanding, an ethical and moral understanding, that we have responsibility to each other. And to the degree that we do not revisit and reinforce that sense of solidarity and connection, and instead rely on security for our protection, I believe we actually make our society even less safe. Because we will have the illusion that we will be safe with armed guards rather that recognizing that ultimately the only thing that keeps us safe is this moral connection. Now this it is not something that you can easily enact into law. The origin and source of this kind of solidarity are not found in law. They are in, again, our civic society. And that's where I think we need to search for solutions and ask ourselves what it takes to rejuvenate those kinds of bonds in our society and in our communities.

Medina: There is a question that I ponder many times and it is: when we talk about education, many times we talk about the learning of certain skills or certain knowledge, certain concepts. But we rarely talk about what you are mentioning here, that is this sense of trust, this sense of connection. We talk about creating and many times are worried, rightly so, about trying to measure what we are doing. But at the same time, I don't know how much of our effort is targeting what we really should be doing.

Noguera: You know, that's an important point. What does it take to reinforce and rejuvenate this sense of trust? Just this week, many in the audience may know, there was another school shooting in New Mexico. A little boy, eleven years old, shot two children around the same age. But what was most interesting about this incident was that his teacher approached him fearlessly and just told him to put down the gun, and he did. I would suggest that, without knowing a lot about the individuals or the background, his willingness to listen to the teacher is probably evidence of some degree of trust he had in that teacher. So it's there, but what is missing is a clear sense of how we build on that and allow those feelings of reciprocity and trust to grow and to come into places when they are needed.

Medina: Being in a school in Boston, one thing that was very striking to me is that after the Boston bombings, the immediate reaction of people was to get together. Soon enough—after a while, obviously—we started criticizing even that fact of getting together. Which I think highlights something that I have heard you say before, which is that in these moments, in these very dramatic moments, you see a perspective of our humanity that is very different from what we usually talk about. In other words, even in the shooting you are referring to today, what made the difference in that moment was something that we never talk about. We never talk about—with teachers, for example—how do you trust, how do you build a relationship with a student? Instead, we talk about what you should be teaching, and how to measure it. To me it sounds even more surprising to see that many times, when you talk to teachers about this aspect, we have a perception that this is not a part of our job. That our job is to expose you somehow to some knowledge that I have, that I have collected over the years. But it is surprising to see how, in these dramatic moments, we see a different side of us that we actually glorify many times, and that I see as not related to a civic commitment. I say this because I see it in Boston, I see it with people of different faiths, I see it with people of many different backgrounds. There is this sense of wanting to be with you in that time of drama.

Noguera: Yeah. It's there, and I think the fact that, during those moments you described, like the marathon in Boston, when people rise to help a stranger that they see in need, we are reminded that the potential for acts of humanity, for altruism, are there. That they are laden in our society gives me hope that there is something, a resource that we could tap and that could in fact produce a more caring and more just society than the one in which we live right now. Schools are central to that work, because schools are places charged not merely with educating and providing skills, but with socializing and preparing the next generation to become adults. I think we have always understood, but have often forgotten, that central to this work is the imparting of values: teaching young people how to become members of our society, members of this community as adults.

I often remind people that if a student gets high test scores but gets strung out on drugs, then we still have failed. If he gets high test scores but ends up robbing banks, even if they are the CEOs of the banks, we have still failed. Because an education without an ethical foundation is an education that produces monsters who will perpetrate acts of injustice against other people. So the real question is: how do we revive that? I am reminded of the fact that Emile Durkheim, the French sociologist, talks about the importance of moral authority. Moral authority, not just in school, but in society, is not based on your title, but is based on relationship. I would bet that the teacher in New Mexico, the one who was able to get the student to put down the gun, had moral authority in the eyes of that student. She was someone he felt he should listen to. Carolina, I know you are a teacher working in Boston. I would say that if the only thing that makes it possible for your children to listen to you and to comply with your requests is fear, then you can never manage a classroom, right? Because you know... but you are not that fearful, right? You are not that intimidating…

Moderator: Ask the kids.

Noguera: The kids...but I bet some of them are larger than you, right?

Moderator: Oh, yeah.

Noguera: So we can't rely on fear and intimidation to get people to do what we want. We have to rely on a higher source, and that's where this idea of moral authority and the ethical foundation for our relationships becomes so important.

Medina: And I like your insistence on relationships, and I like your insistence on the fact that education is about relationships. When we don't highlight that aspect, we fail at teaching. The question that I have, though, is how is it possible for a culture like our modern culture, so self-centered, so insistent that I am my achievements, to perceive relationships as important?

Noguera: Yeah. That, I think, is a critical question for this country in particular, because we have a way of deifying the rugged individual, the triumph of the Bill Gates-types, the individual who is able to amass great wealth and become a titan of industry, and we look up to these people because they have power. We overlook the fact that what ultimately makes our society coherent, what makes it safe, what makes it just, is not the powerful individual but rather the ordinary people who do all the work: people whose works and efforts at raising children and producing the things that keep our society going have to be rooted in an ethical foundation. And so these are competing values, right? The individual versus the community, the collective. And I think that what we have to do is remind people that it is our tension toward the collective, toward the public good, toward our common interest, that ultimately will make the society sustainable. This, I think, is a critical issue for us right now.

Moderator: I am very interested in this last idea. You mentioned that those two competing values exist, so we would have to have a public value that is stronger than individualism. And, in some ways, I know that you have done some work on it. I think it's called "Project for Common Humanity" at NYU, and I am interested in what the common good is and what our common values are. Because it seems to me that we would have to make a very strong case for those in order to debunk individualism.

Noguera: We must recognize that we are in a state of crisis regarding connections, that our society is frail because our bonds to each other, our sense of obligation, is diminished. More and more Americans live alone, live in isolation, and our most vulnerable people, the elderly, the children, the homeless, are in danger because of this isolation. At the same time, we now have good research showing us that there is a human quality, practically genetic, toward altruism, toward the pursuit of togetherness. Rather than to rugged individualism, human beings have been drawn to the collective. This was actually something that troubled Darwin, who gave us the idea of the survival of the fittest. He also knew that human beings, unlike many species of animals, create families, and that in many cases, though clearly not all, fathers actually stick with their offspring. Darwin couldn't explain why would they do that if life was simply about individual interest. Why would humans do this? I would say that now we have evidence from other sources—anthropology, even genetics—which shows us that this is also a part of the human condition. What I am trying to show is that what we need to do is to support and feed that. Consider an issue like global warming. Global warming can be stopped by individuals, right? There are individuals who may be able to erect barriers to protect their homes, but if we delude ourselves in thinking that protecting our individual homes will save us, we will all drown. We need to think collectively about how to respond to the challenge that is facing our society and is facing the world, and that is the reason why figuring this out—how to tap into those innate feelings of reciprocity—is so critical to our survival.

Medina: The question that I have is whether I could push your statement to the point of saying that, as an individual, I need the other in order to be fulfilled. And I say this because it would be a statement that flies in the face of modern society, which basically says that, as an individual, what I need is myself. But this sense, which you say is almost genetic, this sense of wanting to help, I would push it to the point of saying: without the other—and obviously I see a religious connection here—without the ultimate Other, I cannot be fulfilled. Therefore, I see that a society cannot be built, that a community cannot be built without an ultimate—let's put it this way—individual reference to another.

Noguera: Yeah, yeah, I agree completely. We have evidence to show us that this is true, long-standing evidence: for example, people who are isolated and alienated, even with wealth, are much more likely to commit suicide than people who are connected to families, or who are married. And it goes on, beyond that: they report higher feelings of happiness through those connections. A colleague of mine did a study in Chicago. There was a heat wave, and during this heat wave many people died, older people. But he started to study the pattern of where they died, and what he found is that in certain neighborhoods the deaths were much higher than in others. What he discovered, by studying what was going on in those neighborhoods, was that in the neighborhoods where older people were isolated, they died in droves, because nobody went to check on them, to see if they were getting air, if they could breath, or to take them outside. In the neighborhoods were people lived with their families, people took the old grandma and said: "You need to go outside and get some air." Because they were living amongst each other, they were taking care of each other. And so we have lots of evidence that these kinds of family and community ties, of extended neighborhoods, are vital to our survival. However, we still have to address the fact that in our society we don't value this to the degree that we should.

Medina: I would say the reason we don't value this is because ultimately our society is based on the idea of individualism. One of the big questions I always have is: how are we ever going to be able to teach these values? Humanly speaking, when the Boston bombing happened, I perceived my humanity. I perceived the desire and the need to be with others, to pray with others, to accompany others. I perceived the fact that there is a sort of healing within me, a level of humanity that is very different from what I do every day, which is thinking about what I have to do instead of thinking about this sense of connection, this sense of meeting something that is not me. How do we actually change our schools, aware of these facts, and aware that every time I, even myself, get into the classroom, my somehow default position—which is not my natural position but my default position—is to worry about kids achieving, worrying about my job getting done, instead of worrying about truly connecting and truly living.

Noguera: I am glad we brought it back to schools, because I believe that schools are the only institution that is charged with this very important task of preparing young people for adulthood. What we have to always keep in mind is that relationships are essential to learning, even to the acquisition of skills. I am sure Carolina would agree with this: you will see a student who is fine with one teacher, but in another classroom is a problem, not doing their work. Why? Because the relationship is not there. The hardest thing to do is to teach a teacher how to build a relationship. I'll give you a short story to illustrate this.

I was working with a school in California and a brand new teacher from Teach for America. Many of you may know of Teach for America. Anyway, she is smart, she is idealistic, but she is inexperienced. And they have assigned to this teacher the most difficult classroom. She comes to me and says, "Pedro, I need help. My students are giving me trouble. Would you please come and sit in and give me some pointers?" I said, "I'd be happy to." I sit in the classroom and after few minutes it's clear this room is out of control. Kids are screaming, she is screaming, no learning taking place at all. One of her students turns to me and says, "Can't you get rid of her?" I wait till the end of the period and say, "Well, this is bad," and she says, "I can't take it anymore. I leave every day with a headache. I am about to quit." I said, "Don't quit. Let's go together to talk to the principle and explain to him what's happening." So we do, and he listens. Then he says, "You are a professional, deal with it." I speak up and say, "Listen, if you don't help her, she will quit and it's only March. You have to get a substitute for the rest of the year." So he says, "I don't want that." Then he says, "OK, I have an idea. We have a veteran teacher who has just retired. She is very good with children. I am going to ask her to take over your classroom for just two days. I can only afford two days, but I want you to watch her, because she is very good at working with children." So both the new teacher and I think, This is an interesting idea, we want to see what this veteran teacher can do.

The next day she shows up and she's an older woman. Big coat, big bag, something about her walk, something about the look she gives—but the children can tell right away the real thing is here! So the classroom is calm and she starts to teach, no disturbances. The new teacher and I are shocked, 'cause we were there just the day before and it wasn't like that. But at one point during the lesson she sees two girls talking. She stops what she's doing and says, "Young lady, when I'm speaking I want you to be quiet." She turns to the board to write, and under her breath the girls says—please forgive the language—she says, "Bitch!" She didn't say it directly, kind of under her breath. You can pretend it was a sneeze, or a burp, or something else, but this is a veteran teacher. She turns to the girl and says, "Young lady, do I look like your mother?" The whole class did what all of you just did, they all went, "Whooaahhhh." So the girl immediately says, "No, you don't look like my mother." The veteran teacher says, "Well, whenever you speak to me, I want you to think of your mother." With that, she goes right back to the lesson and the class does not miss a beat.

The new teacher turns to me and says, "How did she know that would work?" That's the question: what does this veteran teacher know that the new teacher doesn't know? First of all, she knows those kids know better, they know they are not supposed to act out, they know they are supposed to be learning. She knows that she cannot exacerbate the situation. If she says to that girl, "Your mother is a bitch," what happens now? Now this degenerates into name calling. If she gets on the phone and says, "I need a dean, they are cursing at me down there," what does it say? It says that she is so weak she cannot even maintain order. So what does she do? She says, "Speak to me the way you would speak to your mother." She calls for a different kind of relationship in just that word. And then what? Then back to work. Back to work because she knows that if these children are intellectually engaged, there will be no more disturbance.

Now I would say that's a master teacher. She is a master because she understands not only the content, how to do the pedagogy, but she also understands how to build a relationship. That is what we need to demonstrate to teachers. How this comes together is not about trading off the intellectual work for the relationship, for they go together. But what's hard to do is to teach teachers how to build those kinds of social skills so they can be effective with our children.

Medina: Which highlights the fact that our crisis is ultimately a crisis of society.

Noguera: Yes.

Medina: If our kids are lost it is because the adults are lost; it is not because the definition of the youngsters is to be lost. Actually, and I like it in your example, the default position of a young person is to be in search of, and what they need is to find someone who is an adult. It is a lot of work understanding the fact that deep within us there is a need for relating to things that are not us.

Moderator: Are you asking, more or less, how to create...if not moral people, then at least adults who are bought into a system where they are not supposed to be individualistic and success-driven? As a teacher, I think this is an interesting conversation because our quality or our effectiveness is measured on what our students can produce; rarely is it measured on who we are as people and what we communicate to them in the relationship. So I'm wondering, just from your experience of looking at schools, what does it mean to create or to change adults? How do you change society from that point of view?

Noguera: I would say that like the children, the adults have to be part of communities, and that the faculty has to function as a community that supports each other. It was actually brilliant on the part of the principal, even though I don't like to give him a lot of credit, to know that what this new teacher needed was to see and then to be mentored by a veteran who knew what she was doing. Because in their relationship there will be greater strength for the new teacher. Our teachers need that kind of support. Why do we think that our brand new 25- or 22-year-old teacher should be able to handle children who are often only a few years her junior? That's not possible in many cases, and we are making it way too hard when we know that there are people out there who have figured out how to do this work.

You were talking earlier, Carolina, about how hard that first year was for you, because you thought you could just inspire them with ideas. I would imagine that what has changed for you as a teacher is that you are much better now at quickly building that relationship with your students. Because when children know they can trust you, are safe with you—and safety is critical because in order to ask questions, in order to learn, I have to know that you are not going to humiliate me, that you are going to show patience and compassion in teaching me—things change. Those are qualities that I think lot of times we lose sight of.

Medina: If we want to do this, we have to change the way we think of our education. In this sense, even in the example that you are giving, there is immediately the temptation to say, "I just have to observe this person and do as she does." What we are talking about is that the only way you are going to learn to have that relationship with those students is if you are in a relationship. And I go back to the same thing that I was saying before: if relationship with another is not this sense of openness to the other, is not one of the things that is driving us in life, then we will always apply this sense of it being all about our success, our capacity, about us building ourselves. How do we actually make this our common conversation?

Noguera: That's a good question. I think for me, in my experience, it comes from reminding people of the essence, of what's the most important aspect of this work. This is the reason why, when I said a while ago, "If the children get high test scores but get strung out on drugs we failed," I think most people agreed. Having smart people who are strung out on drugs is not a good thing. And I think that most people do agree that it is essential that we produce a well-educated society. We want a society that is ethical, a society where people are grounded in values of compassion. What we have to do is built that, and remind people that that is what matters most.

Another story, if you will allow me. I was being given a tour of a school, an elementary school also in California, and was being led by the Vice Principal. He was very proud of all the new computer rooms, the new library. We got to his office and a little boy about this tall was waiting for him. And he turned to me and said, "You see that little boy? There is a prison cell at San Quentin for that little boy right now." And I said, "How do you know?" He said, "His father is in prison, his brother is in prison, and I can tell by the way he behaves right now that he will one day end up there, too." So then I asked, "Given what you know about this little boy, what is this school doing to keep him out of prison?" And he looked at me, surprised, because he doesn't think that's his job. In fact, what he was about to do was suspend this student for a month and send his homework to his sick grandmother, who he knew could not supervise, much less teach, the little boy. So when our faculty washes its hands of the student, what we have to do is remind the educator that it is their job to keep the child out of prison. At the bottom line, it is their job to care for that child, it is their job to get to the roots of the behavioral problem, not mainly to punish but to address the character of the child. That is central to education.

Medina: But where do we base this sense of moral authority at the end? When we say that there is a need for this moral authority, where does the school get rooted so that they can communicate this? The reason why we got connected was precisely because of this interest in seeing how the schools are now the tool to create a society. But if we are not content with the society we have, then where are the schools going to be rooted?

Noguera: I think that it really requires a different paradigm, or a different vision of what it means to create schools for the purpose of creating a more just and equitable society. It is interesting: here in New York City the mayor, De Blasio, just appointed the new chancellor, Carmen Farina. One of the first things she said was, "My mission is to restore a sense of hope to schools." Now I was very struck by that, because I would say the paradigm we have been under for the last 12 years has been one of fear. Fear is a powerful motivator: fear of failure, fear of having the school shut down, fear of losing your job. But it is interesting how fear often results in people doing extreme things to avoid the punishment—cheating, for example. We have seen a lot more of that in recent years. Or gaming the system; you know the ways. I am encouraged by a chancellor who, even though she hasn't yet spelled out what this paradigm will look like, recognizes that hope and inspiration are essential to creating schools that will succeed, particularly with our most disadvantaged and vulnerable children. If there is no hope for those children, they will continue to drop out in droves.

Medina: Where do we root the hope, though?

Noguera: You answer that one!

Moderator: This is very interesting to me, because you mentioned earlier that the moment I probably became a better teacher was when I learned to have a relationship with students. Actually, the moment when I became a better teacher was when I developed a relationship with Fr. José. The reason why I am bringing this particular example up is that I learned how to have a relationship by being in one first. Going back to the issue of hope: hope is going to have to come through a very powerful experience. So, not only where does hope come from, but how do you ensure everyone has that experience?

Medina: They are different relationships, just to be clear. It might be confusing at times.

Moderator: This is my father, the other one will be my husband, just to be very clear. The reason why I am bringing up this particular example is that I learned how to have a relationship by being in one first. Hope is frequently going to have to come through a very powerful experience for most people. So, not only do we have to ask where hope comes from, but we have to ask how we ensure that everyone has that powerful experience.

Noguera: Again I think your example is telling. It was relationships that actually helped you to become better as a teacher. You couldn't do it by yourself. You are very smart, talented, committed—but even with those qualities, by yourself you struggled, you needed the support of colleagues and mentors to become better. These relationships are vital to our success as individuals. I remain a very hopeful and optimistic person—and it's not because I am naïve; I am very pragmatic, I am very aware of the huge challenges we face—because my faith rests in God, but also in a belief that human beings do have that capacity, a God-given capacity to solve problems, and to draw upon our strength to try a different course. I still believe that to be the case. I still see evidence that this is the case today.

Medina: The thing that makes me laugh a little bit is that if you go anywhere in public and say that the solution to the problem of violence in our schools is hope, people are going to laugh in your face. It's like we don't realize that appealing to our humanity, this appealing to who we truly are can be a path out. We were talking about this before, and this is why I really like working in the inner city, because when life is difficult, you get to see more of what we really are versus what we do all of the time. But I think it is critical to bring it back to the public square in this sense, because otherwise we will continue to create tools, thinking that they are going to give us this sense of possibility, when they don't. One of the things that struck me very much when I was a principal was—in reference to Facebook—this promise of connectedness. You can have friends on the other side of the world! But this has become the biggest nightmare for educators nowadays, because before, kids were bullying each other but at least they were doing it physically. Now we don't see it, but it is happening. So, I wanted to hear a little bit from you: how, in your personal and professional life, are you actually dealing with starting from a place of hope versus starting from a place of, "Let me tell you what you have to do."

Noguera: I would say that rather than laughing at me, people often...it resonates. And the reason why is because I give concrete examples that illustrate it. A few years ago, there was an incident in Fall River, Massachusetts. A girl approached her teacher and said, "I like you and I have to warn you. Tomorrow, something bad is going to happen here. So, I would suggest you not come to school." The teacher didn't know what to do with the information, but she just thought, Maybe I'd better tell somebody. She told the police, who investigated, and discovered that the girl was part of a group that was planning to shoot up the school the next day. Literally, the relationship between that student and that teacher saved the school.

I went to Columbine High School after the shootings and interviewed some of the teachers and counselors. I asked them, "Didn't you notice these boys in the trench coats, giving Nazi salutes? Why is it that no adult ever intervened?" One of the counselors said, "You know something, we didn't intervene because we didn't think of these kids as at-risk youth." I said, "What do you mean by that?" "Well, they were doing fine academically. They came from middle-class families. We thought they were strange, but we didn't think of them as at-risk kids. So, our time was spent on the at-risk kids." And what this is a reminder of is that lots of us are at-risk, lots of children are at-risk. And they're at-risk because of alienation. They're at-risk because of this disconnectedness. Ultimately, what would have saved schools is knowing our children. Who's at-risk? Who's being cyber-bullied? Who's being threatened? By knowing these things we are in a much better position to intervene and address it, rather than letting children work it out on their own, often without the tools to do so. I would say that what we need to continue to impress upon people and the public is that this work of building these relationships is not airy-fairy stuff. This is real. It is concrete. It actually has an impact on our lives.

Medina: But we are asking teachers to become parents.

Noguera: The law calls for it. It's called *in locus parenti*, right? You are the parent in the absence of the actual parent.

Medina: I wonder how the parents in the room feel about that.

Noguera: I hope they feel good about it.

Medina: Ultimately, how do you learn to do that?

Noguera: I think that we need to spend time. I'm at a university where we train teachers, and I'd say sadly that it's something we pay little attention to. We focus on content knowledge, on pedagogy. We spend almost no time on how you build relationships with children. And I would say that is a huge mistake. In medicine, we've come to realize that if a doctor is highly skilled but can't communicate with the patient, has no bedside manner, that doctor could be totally ineffective in serving their patients. It actually impacts health outcomes.

I think that the same thing is true in education. If you can't build those relationships, you will be ineffective as an educator. This is not a new idea. We wrote about these things. It's been in our culture for a long time. But we lose sight of it, particularly now because we have so much anxiety about our position in the world, about the fact that we are slipping in comparison to so many other countries in science, in math, in reading. And it's true. It's not to say that we shouldn't be concerned about the skills our children are acquiring. We must be. But the social skills are just as important. I recommend a book called *How Children Succeed* by Paul Tuff. What he does is he looks at this literature and cognitive science and finds, increasingly, that it's less about the cognitive ability, and more about certain attributes, non-cognitive skills such as persistence and social intelligence, the ability to form relationships, and to problem-solve with others. These kinds of attributes are ultimately more predictive of success than test scores.

Medina: And the question that I know you are researching is—even though it is probably not the right way to frame it—how do we teach this?

Moderator: Actually, we have been working on this question together.

I think that my boss is in the building. She and I have been working on this. We've developed, or tried to develop, a curriculum to teach character. So this is great because we're trying to teach stuff like grit, and curiosity, and persistence, and all of this stuff that we know has better outcomes than just the cognitive abilities. But what we're finding is that when we're telling adults, "Hey guys, go teach these kids about grit," the kids really don't care, and they won't take it from those particular adults. So there's something breaking down between our beautifully well-structured curriculum on character and the actual instruction. I think it goes back to what you were talking about, relationships, but also about being adults who are capable of educating and imparting a kind of parental role. So we come back to this question in a way: What does it mean to look like someone who can exemplify these things? What does it mean to look like a parent? Because in some way, the systems that we've built, elementary as they are, break down. So, a lot of it is individually dependent. I'm wondering how you would respond to that.

Noguera: Sure. Let me describe a school here in Manhattan called School of the Future, where my daughter attended. What's important about this is that she entered high school there right after her mother died. My daughter was actually 12 when her mother died, and at that age really unable to express all of her feelings, the grief, etc. But when she entered ninth grade, she got a teacher who became her advisor. And that teacher established a very strong relationship with her. In her school, every student must do an exhibition. An exhibition is a project that they work on over the course of an entire year. Each year they do this: ninth grade it's history; tenth grade it's science; eleventh grade it's math, and twelfth grade it's language arts. So, in ninth grade, she decided to do her project on the Roman and the Incan empires. She had to explain how these empires rose and why they eventually collapsed. She had to explain the politics, the religion, the history, the culture. She had to have multiple sources. Throughout the year, she was meeting with her teacher on the project. She was writing the project in phases and constantly getting feedback, feedback aimed at improving and refining the project.

By the end of the year, she had a 25-page research paper as a ninth grader. Then she had to present her work to other students and parents and teachers, because it's not good enough to write it: we want to know if can you explain it to others. There are only three grades offered: distinction, competence, or do over. Failure not an option. Now, as a parent sitting out there, not only was I proud to see my daughter, who had struggled as a reader, produce a 25-page research paper; we're talking about grit. You learn grit through the effort of revising, resubmitting. I saw special-aid students. I saw learning-disabled students. I saw a young man whose parents were deaf, who had language skill troubles from living in a home with deaf parents, stand up and deliver his presentation with such eloquence. Even though he stumbled, the audience cheered him on. Talk about inspiration and hope. So, I think that there are ways that we can embed in our practice the building of relationships, the building of skills, and teach grit and all kinds of things that are essential.

Moderator: I just want to thank you for having this conversation with us today. I, for one, have so many more questions than I started with, and in many ways I don't think that the objective of a conversation like this is to close questions. But I am grateful that both of you have opened them for us.

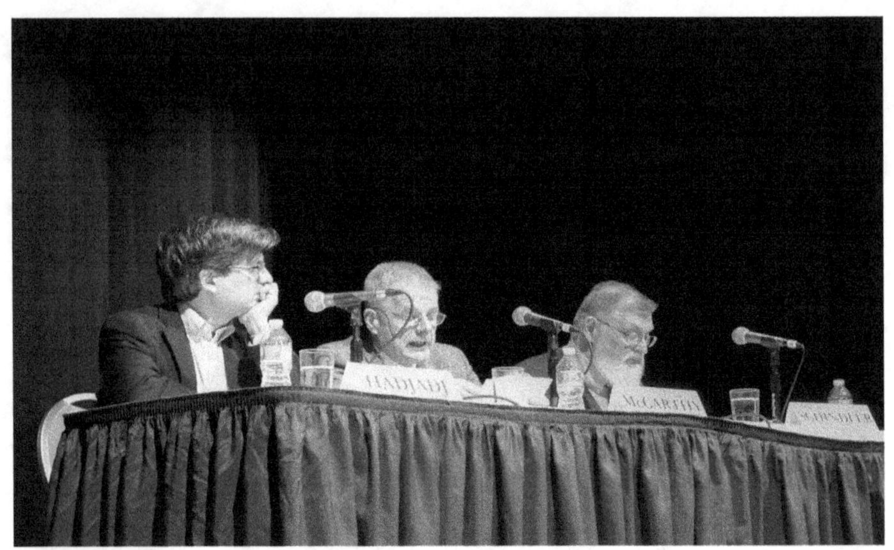
HADJADJ
McCARTHY

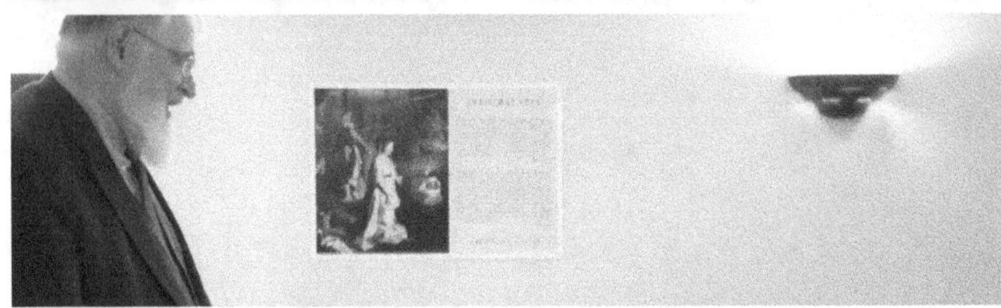

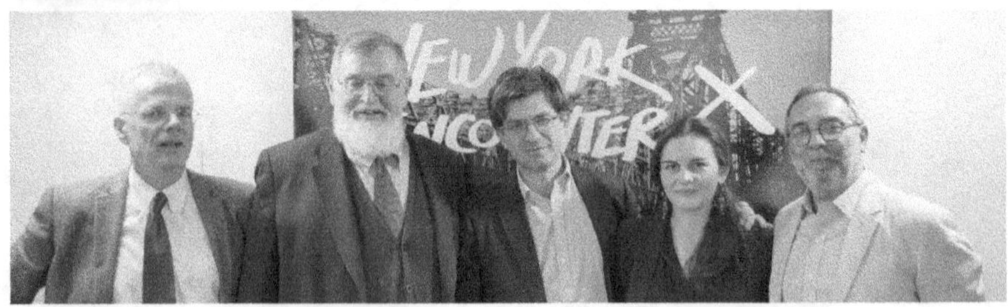

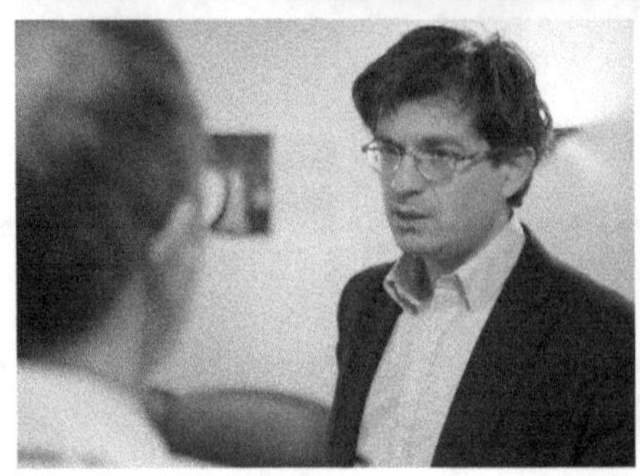

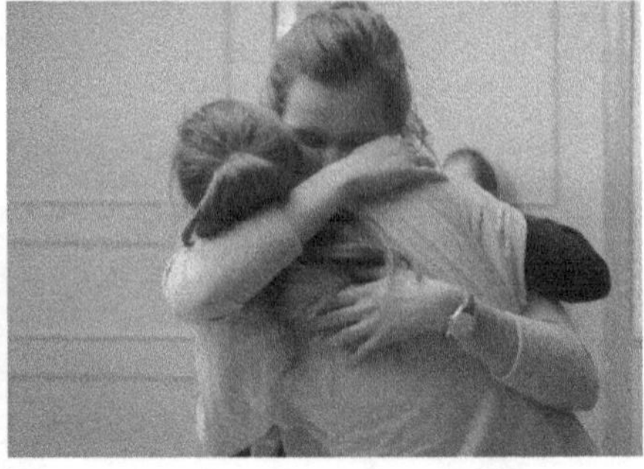

That Hidden Companionship, Stronger than Loneliness

Dr. Fabrice Hadjadj[1] and Dr. David Schindler[2]

Introduction

Nowadays, the debate on what constitutes and defines the human person is very much alive. Can personhood be described in purely biological terms, as suggested by a widespread scientistic approach? Can it be re-created, or even surpassed, by the development of artificial intelligence, as the proponents of a "singularity" predict? What, if anything, makes us essentially different from an ape or a robot?

"The religious sense is reason's capacity to express its own profound nature in the ultimate question; it is the 'locus' of awareness that a human being has regarding existence. Such an inevitable question is in every individual, in the way he looks at everything. The Anglo-American philosopher, Alfred N. Whitehead, defines religion in this way: 'Religion is what the individual does with his own solitariness.'

The definition, although interesting, does not fully express the value of the intuition that gave it birth. True, this ultimate question is indeed constitutive of the individual. And in that sense, the individual is totally alone. He himself is that question, and nothing else. For, if I look at a man, a woman, a friend, a passerby, without the echo of that question resounding within me, without that thirsting for destiny which constitutes him or her, then our relationship would not be human, much less loving, at any level whatsoever. It would not, in fact, respect the dignity of the other, be suitable to the human dimension of the other. But that same question, in the very

---

Saturday, January 18, 2014

[1]Writer and philosopher

[2]Dean Emeritus of the Pontifical John Paul II Institute at Catholic University of America

same instant that it defines my solitude, also establishes the root of my companionship, because this question means that I myself am constituted by something else mysterious.

So, if we wanted to complete Whitehead's definition, then yes, religion is, in fact, what the individual does with his own solitariness; but it is also where the human person discovers his essential companionship. Such companionship is, then, more original to us than our solitude. This is true inasmuch as my structure as question is not generated by my own will; it is given to me. Therefore, before solitude there is companionship, which embraces my solitude. Because of this, solitude is no longer true solitude, but a crying out to that hidden companionship.

A suggestive echo of all of this is to be found in the poetry of the 1951 Nobel Prize for Literature, Pär Lagerkvist:

'My friend is a stranger, someone I do not know. A stranger far, far away. For his sake my heart is full of disquiet because he is not with me. Because, perhaps, after all he does not exist? Who are you who so fills my heart with your absence? Who fills the entire world with your absence?'"

(Luigi Giussani, *The Religious Sense*, McGill)

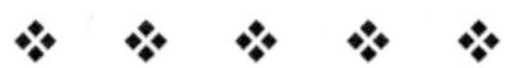

Moderator: Three days after the outbreak of the First World War, an English ship bound for Antarctica left Plymouth Harbor. The ship, christened *The Endurance*, had twenty-eight men aboard. The mission was to make an overland expedition across the continent of Antarctica, a journey of some 1,800 miles. The reason for the mission was in the end quite simple: no one else had ever done it or even attempted it. At the helm was a seasoned explorer named Sir Ernest Shackleton.

On December 5th, the adventurers began the last leg of their sea voyage, setting out from a whaling station on South Georgia, an island roughly 1,300 miles east of Tierra del Fuego. They would never reach their destination. They would, however, accomplish a mission far more daunting than the one they had prepared for. Sea ice came early that year, and their ship was captured by it only a day after sailing under normal conditions from the coast of Antarctica. It soon became apparent that they would now have to wait out the long, dark, and bitterly cold winter, until the spring thaw released them.

Somehow they made it through, but when spring arrived their plight worsened. Under immense pressure from heaving ice, *The Endurance* began to take on water and then started to break up. Shackleton gave orders to abandon ship. Having salvaged the ship's three life boats and whatever supplies and materials they could retrieve, they set out on a long and grueling march to open waters, hundreds of miles away. I won't attempt to summarize their desperate ordeal. Suffice it to say that after more than five harrowing months on ice, capped by a terrifying week in open boats at sea, they reached Elephant Island. For the first time in 479 days, they stood on solid ground, but in a place so desolate and forlorn that there could be no hope of a rescue. Shackleton realized that their only chance was to attempt the impossible.

On April 24, 1916, he and five others set sail for South Georgia in a 20-foot lifeboat, braving 40-foot swells on a sea voyage of 800 miles. Although it's almost hard to believe, they sailed successfully through a hurricane. More astonishingly still, they managed, in what has been described as the greatest feat of navigation in maritime history, to chart the right course by dead reckoning alone. Yet, after 17 unimaginably strenuous days, their ordeal wasn't over. Fearful that their vessel could not handle further battering from the rocks that ring the island, Shackleton decided to make on overland crossing to the nearest whaling station. Without a map to guide them, he could only guess the route up and over the glacier-covered mountains that ringed the island's center. In a state of near-starvation and utter exhaustion, he and the two others stumbled relentlessly on for 36 hours straight.

How they succeeded in reaching the whaling station in such circumstances is something of a mystery. It would take Shackleton another three months before he could return on an ice breaker for the men left back on Elephant Island. Astonishingly, he found every one of them still breathing and still fighting for their lives.

We are gathering over these three days to ponder the question: "What is the human person?" The story of Shackleton and his crew help to remind us just how extraordinary a creature the human person is. Animals just don't do what Shackleton and his men did. Any more than animals congregate in settings such as this one to ask themselves, "What kind of things are we, anyway?" But I recalled the expedition for another reason as well. The present session doesn't seek to impose a philosophical question.

Our speakers will venture an answer, and the answer is that deep down within every human person, within each "I," there exists a You who corresponds to my "I." In other words, however rugged an individual I may think myself to be, or however lonely or alone I may feel, and wherever I find myself, I am never just me. There is always another someone with me, without whom I simply would not exist. And as a witness to this claim I offer testimony from Shackleton himself. At one point, and at one point only, in *South*, the memoir he published about the expedition, does Shackleton make an explicitly religious claim: "Looking back at that long and racking march of 36 hours, over the unnamed mountains and glaciers of South Georgia, it seemed to me often that we were four, not three. I said nothing to my companions on the point, but afterward Worsley, another one of his companions, said to me: 'Boss I had a curious feeling on the march, that there was another person with us.' The third man confessed of the same idea. I leave it to you to decide for yourself to whom they were referring." Shackleton concludes: "The record of our journeys would be incomplete without the reference to this subject which is very near our hearts."

Schindler: Citing the statement of Anglo-American philosopher Alfred North Whitehead, that "Religion is what the individual does with his solitariness," Fr. Giussani insists that, while true, this statement only becomes complete when we recognize that religion is also where the human being discovers his essential companionship. Indeed, Giussani says that companionship is more original to us than our solitude. This is so, he says, because my structure, as question, is not generated by me, it is given to me.
Solitude, then, is no longer really just solitude. It is, rather, I quote: "A

crying out to that hidden companionship, the companionship which is already implied within my givenness as a question." Which is to say, my search for God in my solitariness already implies relationship with God. And it is this hidden relationship in my depths that calls forth my question and sustains my search.

Giussani also refers to the religious sense as the meaning of everything. And, I must say, when I first read *The Religious Sense* many years ago, this was one of the key sentences that always struck me as being at the heart of his genius. The religious sense is the meaning of everything. And he defines reason as the capacity to become aware of reality according to the totality of its factors. So we may say that this hidden community or companionship with God somehow, as a matter of principle, implies community with everything.

So what I want to say a word about, then, is this original aloneness or community with God, and in so doing I want to say a brief word about the meaning of everything. The key structure, my starting point here, is this reference to the structure not being generated by me, but being given to me. And I would like to relate this to that brief statement from Professor Hadjadj in his interview at the Rimini Meeting, when he noted that the word "nature" comes from *nascor*, "to be born"; so in Latin, *natura* means both "birth" and "the nature of things." "Being born," he says, "means to have received existence. To have a nature is to have received at birth a certain structure of existence and not a dynamism, a tendency that is in me and of which I am not the author. That which is inmost in me, returns me to someone other than myself."

So, what I would like to do, then, is focus exactly on that point. Our concern here, our overarching concern, is the nature of the person as constituted in community, as called for in his very singularity, calling for companionship and so forth. I propose that the first meaning of that lies in being born, that is, being from Another, which is to say, being a child. Our first form of relationship has that kind of filial structure, which is a very rich concept. That's the basic proposal I want to make. And since the point here is for a conversation and not just a didactic lecture, I want to briefly record six points that elucidate and fill out what that means and why it's important.

What sense does it convey about nature and the way the person is related? How does it tell us about the meaning of everything? What does it have to do with the religious sense?

Each point is elucidated by the others, so I'm going to be brief. The first point has two parts. To recognize that this notion of childhood actually conveys to us the identity of God—that's the first point I would like to make. In fact, for Christians—and this thought is developed by a lot of people, such as Pope Emeritus Benedict—what we see in the revelation of God, in Jesus, is the eternal sonship of God. That's the first point. In other words, God is taking shape, coming, incarnating Himself through a conception, through a gestation, being born: this is not just accidental to God, but rather it reveals the *Verbum* of God, the Word of God. A lot of times we operate with the assumption that God could have come any way He wanted: He could have shown up in a spaceship, He could have come strapped to, say, one of the Obama Administration's drones or something. The point I want to make here, and it has been developed richly by many theologians, is that in fact the logic of God is revealed in childhood.

Point number one: to be like God. Point number two: all of creation, the meaning of all of creation, especially human beings, is revealed in the sonship of Jesus. That is, we are children in the Child. And in some sense all of being participates in that. We are sons in the Son, we are sons and daughters in the Son. The second point is related to the first: relatedness and being as gift. What I want to say here secondly is that the notion of gift has a primary meaning, and it's in the form of a person. That is to say, the reference point of all gift-giving, ultimately, is the structure of a gift from God: the child. The child, the revelation which takes the privileged form among the various senses of gift—the child reveals what the gifted structure of reality is. And ultimately this is revealed in the Divine Person incarnate in Jesus. That's my second point: the personalization of gift is a child.

I want to make just four quick summary statements to fill that out. What does that imply? How does the child reveal the meaning of the world? That's the first point, and what it reveals about the meaning of the world is that the entire world and everything in it, especially the human being, is from Another—that is to say, created. Again, the paradigmatic form of this—being conceived, being born—reveals the structure of giving and receiving, and is a reference to Another. You can use many different terms, like being as gratitude, that the structure of reality is a matter of gratitude, it's a matter of thanksgiving. Indeed, it's liturgical: ordered to adoration, to giving back what's been given. This goes to the heart of reality.

Now, obviously this is something that has to be examined, because it sounds like poetry. But it's not poetry. People like Karol Wojtyla had some wonderful things to say about this, not to mention Benedict. When Benedict, for example, spoke to the cultural leaders in France in 2008, he chose as his topic monasticism, which is very striking. His point was not only that monasticism really revealed the glory of culture in Europe, but also that it was necessary for the spirit of monasticism, as a necessary condition for any authentic human culture. What is this spirit of monasticism? It's the desire and the search for God and the readiness to listen to Him. That's the meaning of work, and of work as having a liturgical purpose. Ultimately, the revelation of what this means is *Eucarestia*: that is, in Jesus, there is *Eucarestia*.

Second point: the child as the revelation of the transcendentals. We talked about what is true, good, and beautiful—the transcendentals. What do we mean by that technical word, which I use in the classical sense. It means simply that the original meaning of truth, goodness, and beauty is something that inheres in being itself. That being as given is true, it participates in truth, it participates in the good, it participates in beauty. The child is the personalization of truth and goodness and beauty. The child is the personal epitome of what it means to have intrinsic worth, as something given, as something being conceived and born. The very structure of a child is *gift*. It seems to me that you can talk about this in terms of uselessness: it's absolutely fundamental for a child to be useless. They are not really productive yet, but that's the point. It's paradoxical: the child is useless in the first instance because he has his worth in himself, prior to his being useful. So the child's first purpose is to simply be true, to live well, to live the good, to embody it, to embody beauty. The mode of acting that flows out of this is not one of manipulating reality, forcing reality, controlling it and so on, exercising managerial skills and the like. It's a matter of being, of living one's being as true and good and beautiful with the whole of one's being.

That's what the mode of presence is.

To conclude the second point, it's so helpful when we look together at this status of truth and beauty and goodness as given, and how it relates to the status of the child. You will find that they stand and fall together, which seems to me a crucial point. We can see today what has happened to the status of children in our society, a society that has developed an instrumentalist view of reality, where what's true, good, and beautiful can be deemed so only to the extent that it enhances my comfort and improves my estate.

Third point: the child as the revelation of nature and Mystery. What do I mean by the child as nature? The child's nature is something that has at its origin a source of activity within itself as given; it's a sort of receptive originality. The obedience that a child reveals to us is not accidental. There is a relation between the term *natura*, nature, and *nascor*, being born. Being born means being given, as Giussani said, and not being the generator, which means that your being is a matter of obedience; yet it's a matter of obedience creatively. What I want to say in this third point is that we learn from a child, we learn about the meaning of nature and mystery. At the heart of this, what I would suggest in light of the preceding things, is that we need to learn that life is not about the mastery of chance. Life is about fidelity to nature, to a nature at the heart of which is mystery, openness to mystery. Why? Because a child participates in the source that infinitely transcends itself, it has a reference ultimately to what is infinite and to what is eternal.

My fourth point, then, is the question of the child as the revelation of space, time, matter, motion in place, incarnation. *Fiat* conception. We need to ponder these acts as revealing to us the nature of activity, the form of presence, and the way in which presence takes shape in matter, motion, space, and time. That is to say, a conception involves letting be, a forming by, making space for another. An interior presence, to be sure, but a presence of a paying attention with one's whole reality to the whole reality of the other in an ongoing way, which involves undergoing time and indwelling space. There is much that we need to reflect on here. One central point is that space, time, matter, and motion in place are not instruments of presence. They are integral to the form of presence, a presence that would be incarnate: *verbum incarnatum*, word made flesh. That is the way of presence. Taking time, indwelling space, is the way of a living organism, especially a human being, as distinct from a machine.

I read a book recently by Cathy Davidson, and was struck by her argument that multitasking is the ideal mode of the 21st century. Here's the crucial point: she says that attention blindness is a mark of progress. That's her key point. That is to say, because of what we have available to us on the Internet, there is a different mode of presence that can bypass what is incarnate, what takes time, what involves in a profound way being in a place. So, those are my four comments.

I would like to take the occasion to make a final point. You know the issues that are associated with the child: contraception, abortion, mothering and fathering, and today the controversial question of same-sex unions. I want to flag this. Why? Because in the Church, and coming from the top down, there is a concern that we not deal with these questions moralistically. This is a very important concern, and one that's been shared by the last couple of pontificates. The important thing is to see that these issues are, in fact, indissolubly tied to the questions that I was just laying out. That is to say, they are matters of the structure of reality. This is the gift *par excellence*, and requires living a method that lives the "giftness," that is, fidelity to nature that is open to mystery. Abortion, in a way, is obvious; mothering and fathering requires two people who conceive, each of whom makes a distinct contribution; I could go on but will leave it at that. These three realities are not, in first instance, moral issues; they have to do with our relationship to God in a way that it affects the meaning of everything.

Hadjadj: A passage from the Torah, more precisely from Deuteronomy, has always struck me: "The word is very near you; it is in your mouth and in your heart, so that you can do it," (Deut 30:14). This passage expresses something trivial and a mystery. The trivial thing is that, when we read this verse of the Bible, well, the word of the Bible is in fact in our mouths. The passage in question is performative. It accomplishes what it affirms as soon as someone pronounces it. However, its triviality is paired with a mystery: what it affirms refers not only to this sentence; it refers to the divine word itself, entirely—in person, if I dare say so—and it declares that this divine word is always there, present in us. With good reason we can speak here about a hidden companionship—so hidden that what we perceive at first is an absence that drives us to seek that word elsewhere.

We seek transcendence in faraway places, in extraordinary events, and here it is right near us, perhaps too close... I spoke at the outset about mystery and triviality as two contrasting things; now here it would seem that the mystery is precisely the most trivial thing there is, that transcendence is the most commonplace thing of all, and precisely because it is common—being something that has always been there already—it passes unnoticed. Precisely because it is the source of everything that appears—all "phenomena"—it is hidden like the light. Its call is in our very presence. Its spirit is inscribed in our flesh. The passage from Deuteronomy says: "in our mouth and in our heart." I would also add: in our underpants.

I suggest that you do this experiment: contemplate what is found beneath our belt, and discover there a "hidden companionship"; look at the most shamefully carnal part of ourselves and recognize in it the most spiritual requirement. I am not trying to be provocative. I am not the one who is being funny, reality is. When I claim that transcendence is in our underpants, I am being extremely faithful to the Bible. What does the very beginning of the Book of Genesis say? "God created man in his own image...male and female he created them," (Gen 1:27). In other words, the image of God is found in the difference between the sexes. I admit that on my own I would never have dreamed of it. I would have sought what is spiritual only in what is spiritual and not in what is carnal. The Word of God had to reveal it to us. The Word of a Jewish God, by which I mean a God who has a sense of humor.

What I intuited based on the Bible, I would now like to consider rationally. It is enough to meditate on our underbelly, and we cannot help discovering the relational nature of our being. First I see my navel. This is the sign that I did not make myself; rather, I come from other persons, whose family name I bear, too, generally speaking. And if I go a little lower, what do I see? My genitals. And this is the sign that I am not made only for myself, but rather, even in my flesh, I tend, I go toward another. Both the navel and the genitals are connected with sexuality. The latter mark the sexual difference; the former marks the generational difference. The first exists only because we are born of the union of the second.

The difference between the sexes is the one that I would like to dwell on. This difference forms an absolutely original and fundamental relation. In looking at my genitals, I notice that I am a man, and that nevertheless I do not represent all of humanity, because humanity is made up of men and women. I notice also that this member which is at the center of myself eludes my ownership: not only do I not control it entirely—it does not obey my will as my arm does, for example—but also it shows me that my self-realization can come about only through an other, through the other sex, which completely shatters the idol of an individualistic conception of existence.

This is the originality of the relation between the sexes: a relation in which one becomes oneself through this irreducible difference. This originality is often obscured, either by the fantasy of phallic power, or else by the myth of romantic fusion. In the first case, the relationship between the sexes is viewed in terms of domination and therefore of contradiction: one comes to crush the other. In the second case, the relationship between the sexes is viewed in terms of complementarity and therefore of becoming a totality: together, the one sex and the other form a self-sufficient whole. But, as the Jewish philosopher Emmanuel Lévinas showed very clearly, the relation between the sexes is neither contradiction nor complementarity; rather it is openness to the other as other, so that the chasm between them continues to yawn and the other is never absorbed or dominated: "The pathos of love, however, consists in an insurmountable duality of beings. It is a relationship with what always slips away. The relationship does not, *ipso facto*, neutralize alterity but preserves it. The pathos of voluptuousness lies in the fact of being two. The other as other is not here an object that becomes ours or becomes us; to the contrary, it withdraws into its mystery."

The embrace delivers us over to the incomprehensible. The more I embrace the other who is most other, namely the other of the opposite sex, the more incomprehensible that other appears to me. I may penetrate a woman physically, but the woman in her femininity remains impenetrable: she withdraws into a sort of inviolate virginity. And it goes still farther: the otherness of the other is not only preserved and magnified in sexual union; it is furthermore multiplied. By its natural fecundity, this union engenders another other. Sexual difference is never surmounted, except by increasing, in a way, by fulfilling itself in the event of a second unfathomable difference: the generational difference, which gives birth to a child.

Here is the conclusion that I can draw from a simple meditation on my underbelly: I can be fulfilled only with the other and even in the other—not by flourishing but by fructifying; in other words, by giving birth to an other with an other. This is why as long as man exists alone, man does not yet exist. In the second account of Creation, the Eden account, God says: "It is not good that the man should be alone," (Gen 2:18). Whereas the first account of creation in seven days has the refrain, "And God saw that it was good," here God says that, "It is not good." In the second account Adam experiences his solitude, but this solitude, this distress in the paradise of the isolated individual, is the sign that paradise is not in individual well-being, but rather in communion with someone else, a communion that is not a fusion but relation with the one—or rather with the woman—who remains different and multiplies the difference.

If we turn from the origin of biblical wisdom to the origin of philosophical knowledge, we find a similar statement. Aristotle, indeed, sees in sexuality the foundation of man's social nature. The political animal, in his view, is first of all a conjugal animal. In fact, the first natural community is that of the family: it does not depend on a contract, it is inscribed in our flesh; it is not a simple, arbitrary convention but rather results from a necessity without which there would be no society, since there would be no births: "First, then, it is necessary that those who cannot exist without each other couple together, as female and male on the one hand for the sake of generation." This sentence is remarkable, because it mentions two beings "who cannot exist without each other" and who therefore do not really exist unless they are with each other. The one is one only when he is two, and the two are two only if they are more. Sexuality, as fecundity through and for the difference, is the generative principle of all social life.

But it is interesting to note that Aristotle does not stop at that foundation alone. To the genealogical—in other words, sexual—foundation he adds, several lines farther on, a logical, in other words, rational foundation: "It is clear, then, that a human being is more of a political animal than is any bee or than are any of those animals that live in herds. For nature, as we say, makes nothing in vain, and humans are the only animals who possess reasoned speech." The Greek word is *logos*, which can also be translated "word." Man is therefore a political animal because he is an animal endowed with a sex and because he is the animal endowed with speech. Speech is indeed social. As one philosopher puts it: "I talk, but we speak," because speech is always received and addressed. The personal pronoun "I," I learned from someone else, from my parents, and the words that I use are a heritage: I did not invent them. Moreover, I always speak to someone—in this moment, you. The relational essence of speech is found not only in its lexical dimension, it is there also in its vocative dimension.

From this we see that sex and reason, in a human being, are not two juxtaposed realities. Language is at first the mother tongue, my vocabulary and my syntax are initially a patrimony. I was born of the sexual union of my parents, and that is why I speak, not a universal angelic language, but their personal idiom that they pronounced over my crib, and you might even recognize in my voice some of my mother's turns of phrase, certain intonations of my father...

Conversely, human sexuality is spoken. Lovers say to each other: "I love you," and pronounce the other's name with pleasure; spouses promise to live together, and therefore commit their bodies with their minds. We can also observe, more profoundly, that the question "why," the rational question *par excellence*, springs radically from sex. Human beings, as Aristotle again observes, couple in all seasons; they have no particular automatic season. They do not reproduce by instinct, as beasts do, without asking themselves a question. Certainly, sexual union naturally leads to giving life; but, again naturally, man seeks a reason for giving life. Do we lack that reason? Well, then, we will take contraceptives, we will use prophylactics—which never happens with a female dog or a bull in nature. We can even separate sexual union from sexual fecundity to such an extent that the sexual act, instead of being openness to life, becomes nothing more than flight from the anguish of death.

The full deployment of our sexuality therefore requires a hope or, we might say, a valid reason for giving life to a new little mortal. The most physical thing about us demands a metaphysical response. And so, from the dawn of time, human sexuality is surrounded less by ruts than by rites. Marriage, which envelops it, is an institution that is at the same time political and religious. Because God and Civilization—eternal life and collective life—are the only things that provide decisive motives for giving life. Without these motives, one might wonder: what good is it to keep filling up cemeteries? What good is it to have children, if it is only to delay the triumph of the dust? So it is that sexuality drives reason to turn toward something more transcendent. It turns us toward the other sex and, thereby, toward the other child, and in turning us toward the other child it turns us toward God, at least toward a Principle that causes us to hope for life and joy for those who come into the world through us.

But there is an even more profound connection between sex and reason. Aristotle suggests it when he says that, "children are to their parents as effects are to their cause." The first principle of the intellect is the principle of causality: to know something, according to Aristotle, is to know its causes. From the perspective of reason, sexuality is a particular case of causality: children come from their parents. But from the perspective of concrete existence, this causality of generation is the first causality experienced carnally and symbolically, so that one may suppose that any trouble in filiation can cause some trouble in rationality. In order to protect themselves against this double trouble, which would affect humankind in its twofold root—sexual and rational—human societies have instinctively, as it were, established a taboo: the prohibition against incest. To forbid incest, to forbid that a father should lie down with his daughter, or a son with his mother, is to forbid the confusion of effects and causes, and thereby to allow discernment, distinction, the real relation in the difference that is under consideration—in short, reasonableness. The logical order and the genealogical order are entangled; each implies the other.

But there is still something more: sexuality is openness to the other as other, without ever reducing him to oneself. Now this definition holds also for reason. The big difference between human intelligence and animal "intelligence" is that however well it may perform, animal intelligence remains caught up in the circle of the interests of its species. Human intelligence, on the contrary, can be open to anything whatsoever, uselessly, gratuitously. Hence its infinite capacity for discovery but also its perpetual danger of being dissipated. I know a man who is an expert in the science of brewer's yeast: he does not seek to exploit it in a way that would be profitable for humanity; the life of these one-celled creatures is his passion and he never tires of contemplating them for their own sake. I know also a woman who is committed to protecting black tunnel-web spiders: she loves them, she finds them beautiful, she caresses them with her fingertips. Just as through sexuality, in principle, the man turns toward the woman without being able to reduce her to himself, so too by his intelligence a human being turns toward reality without bringing it back to himself. He is drawn toward what is outside, toward objectivity.

By now the reader can guess why, according to Genesis, male and female human beings are made in God's image. What is most spiritual finds its image in what is most carnal, because sex is like the mind—relation to transcendence, to the other in his or her mystery. So much so that for us, unlike angels, sexuality is the basis for our openness to reality in its peculiarity. Through sex I discover in my own flesh the call of the other, and in my own heart the essential "why" question: why give life?

It is not for nothing that Jewish men inscribe on their genitals the mark of the Covenant with God. They thereby manifest this hidden companionship, namely, the fact that transcendence is already in our underpants. The circumcision is in effect the explicit sign of the presence of the completely other in my body—a sign, moreover, that shows itself paradoxically in an absence of skin. And this sign is at the same time the profession of our belonging to what transcends us, and the promise that openness to life is not vain, that giving life to a mortal is not senseless.

Before the creation of woman, Adam names the animals. But he still feels lonely. The companionship that he desires without knowing it, that can open him fully to transcendence, remains hidden from him. Then God makes him fall into a deep sleep and fashions woman out of his side. When he awakes and sees her, Adam not only names her, he cries out and sings: "This at last is bone of my bones and flesh of my flesh; she shall be called Woman, because she was taken out of Man," (Gen 2:23). He discovers his own name, "Man", *ish*, from the name of the woman, *isha*, and he makes this discovery in an acclamation of praise. The sexual difference turns him toward the other in her adorable, marvelous mystery. This shows the most profound dimension of speech and of thought, a dimension inseparable from love: to think is not in the first place to calculate and control; quite the contrary. To think is to give thanks for the presence of the other: to think is to thank...

Moderator: Sometimes there's a deep truth in clichés. So, if you invite a Frenchman to speak, you should not be surprised that he speaks about sex; or that when you invite a grandfather to speak he speaks about babies. There's beauty all around us.

Hadjadj: That's the proof we believe in incarnation.

Moderator: At a certain point in his talk, Professor Schindler insisted that what he was talking about was not poetry. And there's a remarkable agreement between the Frenchman and the grandfather. There is great syntony between the talks. So the objection, the question, that you could put to Professor Schindler could also be put to Professor Hadjadj, and it's this: if you claim that every child manifests the triune God, that every child is the God display, a paramount display of truth, beauty, and goodness—then what about the children who are abandoned in the streets, the children who don't make it out of their mothers' wombs because they are sliced up by a scalpel, the children who have leukemia and suffer horrible deaths, the children that are run over by tyrants, the children who are taken over by drugs or whose parents are brutal to them, who fail them? How can what you say be true if these things are true?

Schindler: There are a number of different ways of entering that, but it seems to me that if you bring to that situation an awareness of something like I presented here, as a Christian and so on, you recognize, you have a more profound sense, in fact, of the brokenness. Because you have a richer sense of what the inherent dignity is and therefore you're drawn out of yourself to have more compassion. I mean, I think the mystery of the suffering of a child is contained in the original vow between a man and a woman, the promise they make to love forever. There's a kind of *fiat* there, to let it be, to let it be in accord with nature and mystery, and you deepen this in the context of faith. But the immediate point I want to make is that there is an affirmation of love that gives itself in the procreation of children, and with an interior receptivity to the outcome of that. Suppose the child is born with severe defects. It seems to me that their love, the very grasping of what the meaning of this is, enables them to have already comprehended in some way the possibility of difficulties; and when these difficulties occur, in a mysterious way they draw out a deeper sense of the gift, a more profound sense of the brokenness. In this mysterious way, utterly beautiful things come into being, precisely in and through that brokenness, things that wouldn't have come into being otherwise. I would say that in all forms of brokenness the depth of compassion is greater, and there's a deeper sense reality.

Moderator: Thank you. Professor Hadjadj, you make this claim about our incarnate character, which you link in an impressive way to reason and, not to put too fine a point on it, sex. But here we are speaking into microphones, we have digital everything. Not quite digital sex, but we are getting there. We think that reason looks most rational in formulae and mathematics, in computers. That's where we are most impressed with what reason can do. So...isn't this poetry that you are offering us?

Hadjadj: Those who talk about artificial intelligence forget, of course, the carnal condition of human intelligence. They imagine intelligence as an instrumental power, a means of mastering the world. But intelligence, before being an ability to master and adapt things, is an ability to be open to what surpasses us, to what escapes our control, to what happens to cause a stir. If we imagine the intelligence as the ability to calculate and plan, then machines already have an intelligence superior to ours. But that is because our concept of intelligence is already artificial—I mean, technological. If we recognize that our intelligence is, in the first place, astonished openness to reality, then we have to admit that a machine will never be intelligent. And a machine will never be intelligent in the way a human being is, because it has no sex. Its foundation is not in the place where I think; it simply functions. It is not torn by the desire for the other as other.

Let me remind you something: the great pioneer of artificial intelligence,

Alan Turing, proposed an experimental protocol to determine whether it is reasonable to consider a computer a thinking being. This protocol is quite telling. It consists of two major points. The first point concerns the construction of the computer. It must be the work of a team made up of members of the same sex. Because it is necessary to rule out the possibility of the members of this crew having a child together and fraudulently introducing a new human being under the gleaming hull of the machine.

The second point has to do with the test itself: a competition between a computer and a man. Both of them will have to try to pass for a woman when someone interrogates them blindly. The interrogator does not see, does not hear voices and cannot smell the *odor di femmina*. In this test of artificial intelligence, why try to pass for a woman? So as to be fair to the contestants. A man who merely had to be himself would not need to simulate in the same way as a computer would. Therefore he must simulate something, not just be intelligent. He has to simulate femininity. If the interrogator does not manage to detect plain differences between the abilities of the man and of the computer to pass for a woman, if the interrogator can be fooled as easily by one as by the other, then the computer can be considered a thinking being. This protocol is quite significant. Both in building the machine and in the test it neutralizes sexuality. One can judge an artificial intelligence only in a test in which thought manifests itself without a body and where sex is interchangeable. But then thought loses precisely the sex that causes human intelligence to wake to itself as well as to others. That's quite a difference.

Moderator: I am happy here and, in a way, sad not to be the oldest person at the table. Happy because I don't want to get old, sad because with age comes wisdom. I want to give the last words to the oldest, but also the wisest, man at this table. Professor Schindler, what does it mean for me, for you, for Fabrice, to learn from a child, to be a child?

Schindler: It always struck me that John Locke, in his second treatise, singles out Adam and the privileged status of Adam. Why is his status privileged? He said the key is about Adam: he wasn't born; he's the only human being who wasn't born, so what is the advantage? The advantage is that he didn't have to go through a stage of weakness. He was in complete possession of himself. This operates in his philosophy. The point that I want to make, though, is not that we remain children forever, it's that we retain the memory of childhood in our adulthood. So even though we take possession of ourselves, the inner form is that we are not our own, that we are references to another. We come from another, therefore our being is fundamentally one of gratitude. And we always have to remember that there is an essential Person in God, a key Person who, so to speak, never grows up: He is the Eternal Child. There is something eternal there, and a reason why Jesus says, "Unless you became like a child you can't enter Heaven." It's something we have to retain through our lives, and on this point the view of Ratzinger and others is quite different from that of Locke, and has a lot of cultural consequences.

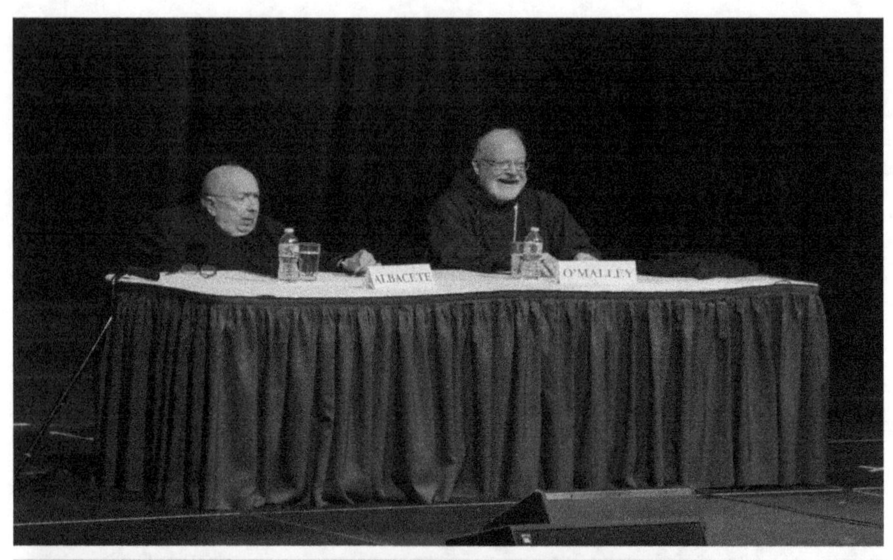
ALBACETE
O'MALLEY

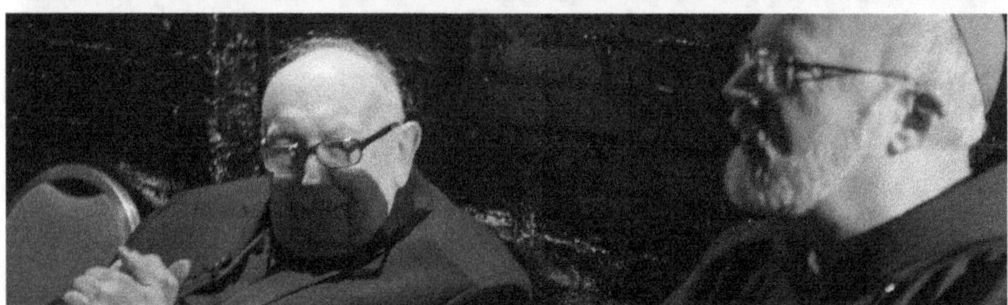

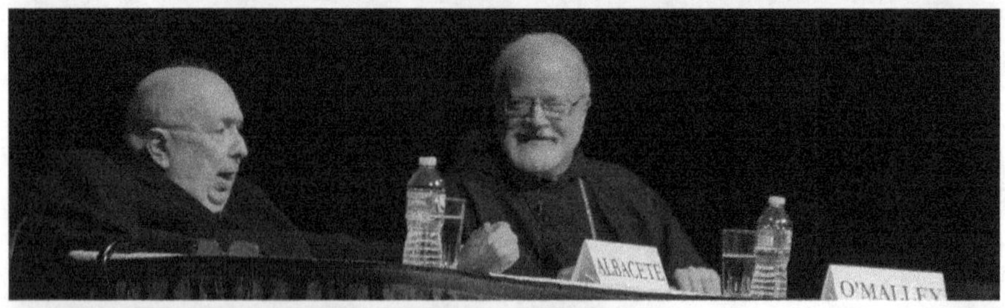
ALBACETE

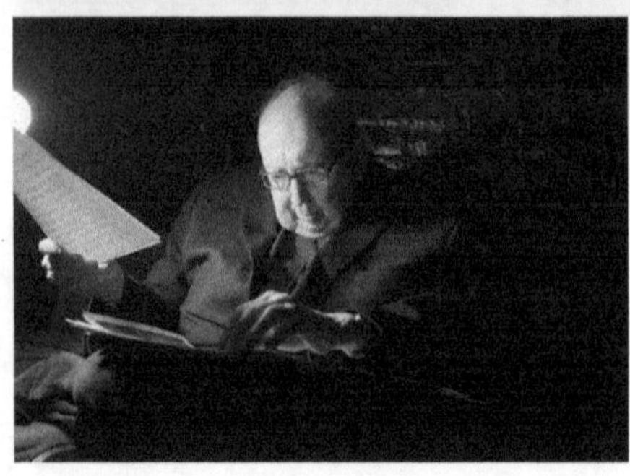

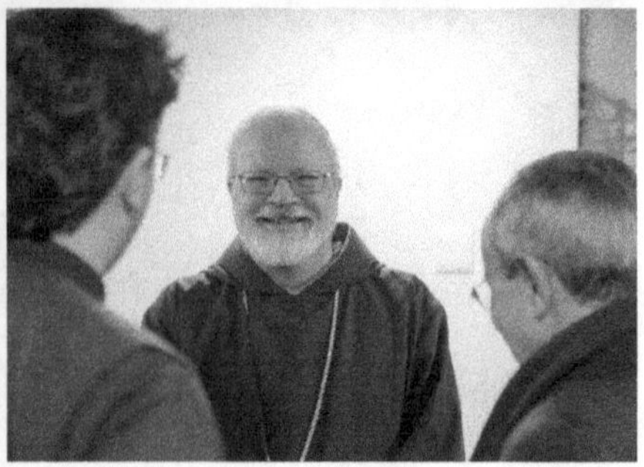

"Go Out, Head for the Periphery" (Pope Francis)

Cardinal Seán O'Malley[1] and Msgr. Lorenzo Albacete[2]

Introduction

"There were 'bad times' under the Romans, too. But Jesus came. He did not spend the years of His life complaining or denouncing the 'bad times.' He cut it short. In a very simple way. By building Christianity. He did not end up indicting or accusing anybody. He saved. He did not indict the world. He saved the world."

(Charles Peguy, *Veronique*)

"A Church which 'goes forth' is a Church whose doors are open. Going out to others in order to reach the fringes of humanity does not mean rushing out aimlessly into the world. Often it is better simply to slow down, to put aside our eagerness in order to see and listen to others, to stop rushing from one thing to another and to remain with someone who has faltered along the way. At times we have to be like the father of the prodigal son, who always keeps his door open so that when the son returns, he can readily pass through it.

Let us go forth, then, let us go forth to offer everyone the life of Jesus Christ. Here I repeat for the entire Church what I have often said to the

---

Sunday, January 19, 2014

[1]Archbishop of Boston
[2]Theologian

priests and laity of Buenos Aires: I prefer a Church that is bruised, hurting, and dirty because it has been out on the streets, rather than a Church which is unhealthy from being confined and from clinging to its own security. I do not want a Church concerned with being at the center and which then ends by being caught up in a web of obsessions and procedures. If something should rightly disturb us and trouble our consciences, it is the fact that so many of our brothers and sisters are living without the strength, light, and consolation born of friendship with Jesus Christ, without a community of faith to support them, without meaning and a goal in life. More than by fear of going astray, my hope is that we will be moved by the fear of remaining shut up within structures which give us a false sense of security, within rules which make us harsh judges, within habits which make us feel safe, while at our door people are starving and Jesus does not tire of saying to us: 'Give them something to eat' (Mk 6:37)."

(Pope Francis, *Evangelii Gaudium* 46, 49)

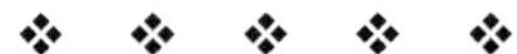

Albacete: I met you about 45 years ago. It has been the longest-running friendship I've had, and there has been no time in which I have not known where you are. Time passes fast. We might not talk every week, and maybe even months will pass between meetings, but I've always felt that you are nearby. However, I have never explored this friendship from any other perspective than that of simple enjoyment. So, the preparation of these questions that I am going to ask you has been an exploration, an exploration of myself, in an attempt to discover what in this friendship has attracted me so much, and sustained this friendship for so long.

We should use this quote of the Pope, in which he says we should leave the center and go to the peripheries now and then, in order to experience what people are experiencing, and to take to them the Gospel so that it may become the center of their lives. Pope Francis uses a language we're not necessarily familiar with in the United States, because "periphery" for him means what we call the inner city. That is to say, the direction is totally reversed. In Europe, as you know, the poor move to the periphery, outside, and those with money and status move to the center of the city.

Here, it works the other way around: the poor take over the center, while the people with resources move to the periphery. So when I say "the periphery" I mean what we mean by inner city. And this is where Cardinal O'Malley flourished, in the inner city. But he flourished in the center, too, and everywhere we went. It is as if he always belonged to where we were. I never felt a conflict between the two.

For example, it is said that the man who sits here owned, or maybe as far as I know still owns, a high-rise building in the periphery of Washington, DC, which cost him...some versions say one cent, other versions say one dollar. He also at one time owned, or borrowed—or stole, for all I know—I don't know how many homes. They were named after Franciscan saints, and in them he would hide people sought by the police. I mean, what's going on? All of this was perfectly harmonious with his Franciscan vocation, his ministry, his sacramental ministry. Most priests go through a very difficult time trying to combine the two, that is, the sacramental aspect of our vocation—to hear confessions, say the Mass, etc.—as well as the help for the poor. He never had such trouble.

So let's try to deal with that question which I think is the most important one facing the Church today—I repeat it again, I think this question is the most important one, facing the Church today: let's find out the true story of the one-dollar building and the houses.

O'Malley: Thank you, Lorenzo. As Monsignor said, we have been friends for over 45 years and that friendship has been a great treasure for me. Lorenzo is a gift to the Church. He is brilliant, and his zany sense of humor is something we all enjoy very, very much, and despite—

Albacete: —See, he says these things, that's why I continue being his friend!

O'Malley: I knew Lorenzo before he went into the seminary. I was a young brother, it was before I was ordained a priest. I was a Capuchin brother in Washington, studying in the seminary, and as a matter of fact it was my privilege to preach at his first Mass, out of the *resulta para me*. Afterwords, his mother, Donna Conchita, had a lovely reception for him in their home, which was a new apartment she had just moved into. When we got there after the first Mass, she said, "Oh Padre Seán, will you bless my new apartment?" And I said, "But Donna Conchita, your son was just ordained." She said, "But I think he's joking."

Albacete: She never really believed I was validly ordained. In fact, on one occasion, using a suspicious Vatican contact, she and my brother were flying with me from Milan to Lisbon. They were terrified of airplanes, but a friend in the Vatican, who later on ended in disgrace, had arranged for us to go first class, to enter the plane before everybody else, to make it as kind and pleasant as possible. Anyway, so we were there: myself, my mother, my brother, and suddenly the regular passengers boarded and there was a whole group of pilgrims to Fatima. And suddenly my mother said, loudly, "Oh look, there are two or three priests with that group! Nothing bad will happen." The flight attendant was standing there and looked at me like, "Who are you?" She never really...I had forgotten about the house.

O'Malley: Well, that's where Lorenzo got his sense of humor. His mother was a very charming and witty person as well.

I think I have to clarify that I never actually owned any property. I am a Capuchin. But we did have a building where we rented the first floor; it was a tenement building in Washington, and we had there the Centro Catolico offices and our clinics. It was a building that was in very bad shape, and at one point the owner decided that he was going to sell the building and evict everybody there. So, we started a cooperative. What the person didn't realize when he tried to sell the building is, in Washington, there's laws that say the tenants have the first right of refusal. And because they neglected to offer us the building, there was some leverage for us to acquire this building and we started this tenants' cooperative. In the building there was a lot of violence, and most of the people were armed to the teeth and there were gun fights going on all the time. At the first meeting of the cooperative, which I held in the lobby, they elected me president, so I put a card table in the center of the room and asked everyone to put their guns on that card table, because the police in Washington had a buy-back program. "You know, they will give you money for the guns," I said, "but more importantly, I am terribly worried that some children are going to get killed," because there really were gun fights going on. And there was sort of a silence after I made this petition, and then this little old grandmother opened up her purse and took out a pistol this big. She waived it under my nose and she said, "Father, you are a priest, no one is gonna do anything to you. Me, I'm keeping my gun!"

Albacete: She was an agent of the NRA.

O'Malley: Not really, but it took us a while to disarm the people there.

Albacete: You know, it sounds really funny that you would be the one doing this, because the entire time you were wearing what you're wearing now: this Franciscan habit surrounded by guns.

O'Malley: That's what kept me from getting shot. But as far as the houses, I do want to say this: for years and years, all of us who are Lorenzo's friends have said that we wanted him to have something like the old Jack Parr Show, which today would be like Jay Leno, something like that, where he could do interviews. I always imagined him interviewing Dick Cheney and Zsa Zsa Gabor; I didn't realize I was going to be his victim.

Albacete: It has come down to this.

O'Malley: He said this is as close to Broadway as we'll ever get.

Albacete: I mean there is even a name for our group. You see, it's very difficult. This is a very difficult thing for me. Because I am awed in the best sense of the word. That is, I am in front of something that is from beyond, from the Mystery, that shines through him. I am not saying that he is the author of it; on the very contrary. But there is a transparency, there is something that I respect a lot. Second, at the human level, it has been wonderful to have a real friend like this. But third, part of it is the funny things that have happened—and he is a very funny man. And humor usually isn't packaged together with the rest of those attributes. We appear before you now as a Broadway act called The Two Bums, a name that he gave our friendship. Why don't you explain to the people why we are The Two Bums?

O'Malley: Lorenzo!

Albacete: It's true. The shrimp...

O'Malley: Yes, well, we were invited to preside at a wedding. I don't remember which one of us preached and which one of us recited the vows. They were a very wonderful couple, and they had the wedding in West Portland in this very fancy place. It was a great reception, where the amount of shrimp consumed by the two clerics was very large. And then Lorenzo says, "Let's go to a bookstore." I said, "If we leave now, they'll say, 'Those two bums ate all the shrimp and left.'" But we went to the bookstore anyway.

Albacete: They didn't even notice we were gone! But then, all of that was a preparation for the big encounter with the poor. I think it was a lady who asked you for money.

O'Malley: Yes, she said, "It behooves you to give me $10." You were very impressed. She was used to that, you know...

Albacete: So The Two Bums appear before you now. You're all very privileged.

O'Malley: Lorenzo, let me say a little bit about the Centro Catolico. I often share this story with people because it gives a sense of what I experienced there, going there as a young priest. When I joined the Order, I thought I was going to the missions, and actually I was told that my first assignment would be on Easter Island. I was learning Rapanui, the Indian language there, when Cardinal O'Boyle, who was our bishop at the time, went to the Provincial and said, "You have a deacon that speaks Spanish. I need him here in Washington." So, my whole life changed overnight because of that.

I became the Director of the Spanish Catholic Center. My first week there was spent working with immigrants—the wars were going on in Central America, Nicaragua, El Salvador, Guatemala—and thousands of refugees were crossing the border, many of them coming to Washington. In Latin

America, in many countries, the capital is the largest and the most important city; so a lot of people, when they think of coming to the United States, they think of coming to Washington, D.C., particularly those people from countries in Central America. Many were crossing the border illegally by means of smugglers, called "coyotes," who would bring them to Washington on a "Go now, pay later" kind of arrangement.

My very first week there, a man came into the Centro Catolico, he was very upset and crying so hard he couldn't even talk, and he gave me a letter to read. It was from his wife. In the letter she castigated him. She said, You abandoned me and our six children, and we are starving and you said you were going to go to Washington and get a job and send us money. He explained to me that he'd been a farmer in El Salvador, but because of the war it had been impossible to conduct his business. So, like many other men in his village, he came to Washington, principally to work in restaurants. The Salvadorians were often working as dishwashers, which they referred to as *gravando discos*, making records.

This man said to me, "Father, I live in a room with several other men. We all came here to be able to support our families. I work in two restaurants washing dishes. I walk to work so as not to spend any money on transportation. I eat the leftovers from the dirty dishes, so that I don't have to spend any money on food, so that all of that money I can send back to my family in El Salvador. Every week all the money that I could earn, I put it in an envelope and I put it in that blue mail box at the corner to send it to my family."

I questioned him and said, "Do you send a check, or a money order?" He said, "No, Father. I always send cash."Then I looked out of the window and saw the blue mail box, which was actually just a very fancy trash bin. For almost a year this man, working so hard, and worrying about his family, was throwing all of his money away.

It brought home to me how difficult it is to be an immigrant, to not know the language, and often to not have documents, to live in that fear, to not know the culture where everything is strange. And that's the population that we were working with. Recently, in the newspapers here in New York, there's been a lot of publicity about an Indian diplomat who was arrested and, unfortunately I think, mistreated. A strip-search for a women like that is outrageous.

But the problem it underscores is something that we lived with in Washington. There were so many embassies to the White House, so many embassies to the Organizations to the American States, many international organizations, the World Bank, the Inter-American Development Bank; all of these organizations had diplomatic status, and their workers were entitled to bring household workers with them and extend visas to them. There was a lot of abuse in that kind of situation, where people brought women from their countries to work as servants in their home. Every week in the Centro Catolico, we would have problems arising from this sort of abuse.

One young woman was brought to be a au-pair—to take care of the children, she thought. She was about 17 or 18. She came with this family, and when she got here she discovered that she was not only taking care of four or five children, but she was also washing the clothes, cooking, cleaning the house, cutting the grass, shining the man's shoes—and this was seven days a week. At the end of every month she would get a receipt saying, "We're charging you so much for your room and board, your toothpaste, your transportation." At the end of three years they had not paid her anything. Luckily, she saved all of those receipts, so when she came to the Centro Catolico I found the meanest Cuban lawyer we could afford and we sued that family, and he came to us—

Albacete: —Who else would know the meanest Cuban lawyer?

O'Malley: So, we sued this family, and the Cuban lawyer came to me and said, "Well, they are offering $20,000 because, you know, they are diplomats, they are immune, so you better take it." So we did. But every week there were these problems, and so often the diplomats would take the passport away from the woman to make sure she wouldn't try to leave or change jobs. And so we did it, we had these houses that some people called safe houses where, if women needed to leave one of these very difficult situations, we would have a place they could stay, with wonderful Spanish nuns working with us, Carmelite Sisters, who ran many of those houses for us. We started a group for the women, a sort of a union for domestic workers. We called them "The International Association of Household Technicians."

And strangely enough—I shouldn't say it, it will scandalize you all. At the time, our mayor was Marion Barry. He was the one who said, "The witch made me do it." But he didn't say *witch*, and all the kids were wearing the t-shirt when he was arrested—but anyway. He appointed me and Gloria Steinman co-chairs of a committee to set the minimum wage for household workers. That was a very interesting experience. We managed to set a wage that was much higher than the regular minimum wage.

However, the problems with the diplomats continued, so when I saw this recent [diplomat controversy], it was sort of a consolation to me, because in the years when I was in Washington, we could never get our authorities to do anything about these situations. They would always say, "Well, they have diplomatic immunity and there is nothing we can do." But to me it was very significant that the Holy Father, Pope Francis, as his very first outing, took a trip to Lampedusa, which is an island off the coast of Italy where many illegal aliens—as we used to call them here in the United States, undocumented workers—try to establish a beachhead, so to speak, to get into Italy and Europe. The Holy Father went there realizing just how much suffering those people experience. I was very moved by the homily that he gave and his remarks. He also threw a wreath into the water where thousands and thousands of immigrants have drowned in their attempts to reach this island of Lampedusa.

In the United Stated right now there is a lot of talk about immigration reform, and there is so much resistance to it. The bishops have been very clear, trying to advocate for a more just system, more just laws. Right now we have so many workers here, millions of people who are in our country, and many of them are exploited and have to live in fear, under the radar. So, when we talk about people on the margins, in the peripheries in our own country, certainly the undocumented workers who are here in large numbers are a very important demographic for the Church. Many of them are Catholics, so we are very concerned about their faith. In the Centro Catolico, most of the people we served were in that situation. Over the course of my 20 years in Washington, I came to realize the great suffering of these immigrants and their great generosity. In many of the countries of Central America, the largest portion of the gross national product is actually the money being sent back from people washing dishes in Washington, working as maids and parking cars in garages, and living very, very sacrificial lives, just to support relatives and friends back in their own country.

Albacete: A superficial thing, which is just a little anecdote. The founder with whom I worked at the John Paul II Institute in Rome, his name is Carlo Cafarra, who today is a cardinal, too; all these people became cardinals, while I became an altar boy. In any case, Cardinal Cafarra is the Archbishop of Bologna these days, but at that time he was the founder of the Institute and would come to Washington periodically to visit us, to give us a talk, maybe to give a little mini-course. I was hanging around with His Eminence here, so they met, and we decided to go out. I can't remember... it was a steak house.

O'Malley: The Sizzler.

Albacete: The Sizzler! Cafarra used to call it "Lo Sisler." Anyway, we went there, and when we entered, the entire kitchen—everybody, the whole mob of people—saw him and cast themselves at his feet, holding on to his habit, saying things like, "Oh consoler of the afflicted." Cafarra looked at Seán and said,"It's the litany of the Holy Spirit." Well, this meeting is still remembered by Cafarra: there is a man among you that came to me a few years ago and told me he was from Bologna. I told him to go and tell Cafarra that he—the man—had seen me, and what we were doing. So now, yesterday, he told me he had gone to see Cafarra and had told him about this meeting. Cafarra laughed and said, "Send my regards to him and to Cardinal O'Malley."

Anyway, that's unimportant, it's an anecdote. But it's an anecdote that has its base not in superficial emotion—because, I repeat again, while all this is happening and we are either crying or laughing or whatever, there is something else there. I see a picture. I saw it when I came to visit you one afternoon at the Centro Catolico: you were in some kind of argument with a government official, when suddenly one of the ladies who were there came and gave you a piece of paper and you left the room. You went to hear a confession. Then you came back and continued the argument with the man. And there was absolutely no change: it seemed you were responding to the same reality, whether arguing with this guy or hearing an old-fashioned confession. That said something to me, and in fact it still does. Because I feel a conflict many times between works of justice that I feel have to be done, and my sacramental vocation. Could you say something about this?

O'Malley: You know, I think you have an interesting point there. In the Centro Catolico, most of the people we were serving were not documented. We weren't in partnership with the government at all. It was an entirely Church-sponsored agency. In the United States, we have this tradition of partnership between the non-profit and government sectors, and it often puts the Church in a position where we're involved in very good social ministry and social services, which are somehow kept separate from the pastoral services. Whereas in the Centro Catolico the two were aspects were joined, we were there to serve the whole person. Pope Francis often says that the poor are not just underserved in the area of social services, but are underserved pastorally, and this is a big challenge for the Church. We were trying, I think with some success, to serve people's spiritual needs as well as their physical needs. We would have English classes, GED classes, literacy classes. But when we had a retreat, or a day of recollection, we would invite all of those people in the classes to attend the retreats.

Albacete: I remember they gave you money. The government would give you money to take care of young people during the summer, to keep them from running around the schools. You use to do it at Catholic University, at the Shrine. I saw you there surrounded by hundreds of kids, and you were in a procession of some kind, some saint, and I said, "What are you doing here? This is a summer program, with processions..." "They don't know." He took their money and then—

O'Malley: —You are going to get me in trouble, Lorenzo! They are probably waiting to arrest me!

Albacete: Then you can visit the jail.

No, but please, what I want to say is that it's not a question of one or the other, either/or. It's the same. Your commitment to the poor, to social justice, is just as much a part of evangelization as is your commitment to sacramental needs. I think the poverty of which the Holy Father speaks is the one that is all-encompassing, it's the poverty of our own selves, without God and therefore without Christ. The commitment to live this, I believe, is what he means by "a Church of the poor." The Church is poor by nature, this is what I want to say. So when you see him, tell him that I said that he should introduce the subject as salvific poverty.

O'Malley: I'm taking notes. The Holy Father's notion of the culture of encounter is something so beautiful. In *Evangelii Gaudium* he talks of reverence for the other, almost like being in the presence of the burning bush, the realization of how precious every human being is. The Holy Father's message has certainly touched the hearts of everyone. It's amazing. It's so basic, just reminding us what the Gospel is about: love and service and reconciliation. The Church's mission is something that all of us are called to become involved in, and it's so different from the individualism of our culture that has resulted in this sort of New Age spirituality: "Jesus is in me," or "I'm spiritual but not religious." The Holy Father's approach completely blows that to smithereens. You're a disciple of the Son of Light, you're part of this community, you're part of God's family—we have responsibilities to each other. And those who are suffering, those who are poor, have a very special claim on our love.

I always tell the story that once, here in New York, Cardinal Spellman was in his office and the intercom rang. It was the new secretary, in the lobby, and she said in sort of a whisper, "Your Eminence, there is a man in the lobby, who says he's Jesus Christ. What should I do?" The cardinal said, "Look busy." Of course, what the cardinal said so glibly is true, because that homeless man, off his meds, that schizophrenic man who thinks he's Jesus Christ, *is* Jesus Christ—as Mother Teresa used to say—"in a distressing disguise." I was privileged to be able to go with the Holy Father to Assisi on the feast of Saint Francis, and it was just an extraordinary experience.

Albacete: I am sure very different from when we went together.

O'Malley: Actually, it was a helicopter ride, and this brings up another story.

My first helicopter ride was with Lorenzo, in the Dominican Republic. Lorenzo taps me on the shoulder and says, "We are running out of fuel." And of course we thought, "This is one of Albacete's jokes." But this was Albacete the aeronautical engineer speaking. When the pilot realized it, we had to make an emergency landing in a field. Cardinal Bauman was with us. Then these very lovely campesinos came out and gave us coffee.

But let me tell you about Assisi. When we arrived at Assisi in the military helicopter, the Holy Father's first stop was at the Istituto Serafico, which is an institution in Assisi run by the Church. It takes care of severely handicapped children. To me, it was just an ingenious way to begin this Franciscan pilgrimage, because Saint Francis' own conversion, which he described in his last testament, took place in an encounter with a leper. Saint Francis had a phobia of leprosy: whenever he saw a leper he would run in the other direction. But this one day he encountered a leper and God's grace touched his heart and he got off his horse. He went over to the leper. He gave him all his money. He gave him his clothes. He kissed the leper, and for the rest of his life he said, "That was the moment when my life was changed, when everything that had been bitter before changed into sweetness."

And so, for the Holy Father to begin his Franciscan pilgrimage by this encounter with suffering humanity, I thought it was such a beautiful gesture. He kissed every child, he spoke to every parent and every caregiver. And then he talked about how the Risen Lord, when He appears and shows his wounds—the Risen Lord is still the wounded Christ. Although the other aspects of the Passion disappear, the wounds are still there. Then the Pope said, "In the Ascension, Christ takes those wounds with Him to Heaven," and, "These children here are those wounds on the body of Christ, those wounds that Christ is going to take to Heaven, and we have the opportunity to worship the wounded Christ in their sufferings."

Albacete: What I want to say is that those very words are not a metaphor, these poor people are not Christ metaphorically, doing it in the name of Christ, doing it remembering how Christ was. They are, in some way, the real Christ. There's no other one. They are His Body now. Otherwise there has been a disincarnation. This is what I have seen in Seán that is so magnificent, because people think of it in a sentimental way, that popularity is due to sentimental things.

Before we run out of time, talk about your vocation a little. If anything has been characteristic of it, it's how a vocation is made up of surprising changes. To make sure you are not going to do something, just want to do it. You plan to do *this*, but no, you are sent to some other place. When you were finally at home, so to speak, working for the care of the Hispanics in Washington, you ended up in the Virgin Islands, where I had to come and help you because you kept driving over people's feet.

In any case, there you were, which is fine because they give you an excuse to go to the Virgin Islands. And there you were having to learn another culture, because no matter how close the Virgin Islands are to Puerto Rico, they are different cultures.

O'Malley: Can I tell them a story? When I first arrived in the Virgin Islands, I was very nervous, because to go from one island to another I had to go on these sea planes and I was just dreading the sea planes. So I went down to the harbor and we were lined up to get on the sea plane, and in front of me was a very large, full-figured West Indian woman. The pilot had a little pen and paper and he said, "Miss, how much do you weigh?" And of course everyone was listening very carefully. She said, "Eighty pounds." He said, "Bishop, how much do you weigh?" I said, "Three hundred." But it was a great experience in the Virgin Islands.

Albacete: But it was not only a change of dioceses; you were not a bishop until you went to the Virgin Islands.

O'Malley: That's right.

Albacete: I remember. I'll never forget this—I haven't even told you before. Of course I did not concelebrate the Mass for the installation, because

I would rather walk around the streets and take pictures and fill the movie camera that I had just bought, and because these things make me nervous. Anyway, I was walking to some place in the building and you were vesting. The door was somewhat open and I could see you putting on bishop-type robes and being very uncomfortable with it at the beginning. But I saw something that wasn't—that I cannot explain even now, that I only saw one other time, the day you were installed as Archbishop of Boston: the combination of receiving a cross and a consolation. The consolation of having Christ touch you, even if it hurts. So many times, those two images brought me the peace I was looking for. And so the Virgin Islands appointment was very important, thank God for that.

In any case, was the Virgin Islands appointment due to the Argentinian military, or something like that? Does the Pope know this? Does he know that the Argentinian military has targeted you?

O'Malley: Lorenzo, you're telling all of my secrets; I'm going to have to go into the Witness Protection Program. We were in St. Matthew's Cathedral, and the Cappella Latina was a chapel in the Cathedral. I worked at the Cathedral for many years with the Spanish-speaking population there, and Lorenzo was a member of that parish for a while. But he's referring to a Mass we had for the Argentine Independence Day. It was right in the midst of what has come to be known as The Dirty War, in which the military dictatorship was in conflict with a leftist gorilla group. In their fight against the gorillas, they were killing anyone who criticized the government.

There were four French nuns, members of my community, and many Passionist Fathers who were murdered. The Holy Father made a statement about it, talking about the dangers of this ideology of the National Security Doctrine, as it was called. So, when I was invited to celebrate this Mass for the Argentine Independence Day, it would have been very difficult not to reference what was happening in the country. So of course I, in my homily, began to quote extensively from the Holy Father's reflections on Argentina. And in the congregation there were scores of Argentine military. This one general got up and said "Fuera!" and everybody ran for the doors, 800 people leaving the church during the homily.

So, I always tell my priests, if you see your congregation yawning during the homily, it's not the worst thing that could happen: they could actually get up and run to the door. I was a young priest, and very worried about the consequences. I was also concerned about the archbishop—I didn't want to embarrass him, you know. But Cardinal Bauman was told what happened, and he instructed Monsignor Quinn, who was the Rector of the Cathedral, "Well, whenever Fr. Seán preaches, make sure that the collection is taken up before the Gospel."

Albacete: All right, I won't let us go out that way. We have to be closing the show. Next subject. In any case, a lot of this running around was understood by many people as somehow related to the crisis in the Church involving the sexual abuse of minors. I remember the year you were moved from the Virgin Islands to Falls River. I remember going to your inauguration with Carl Anderson. We drove over to Falls River and I just sat among the priests of the diocese. You have never seen more demoralized people. Media people were camped outside the church, not just local media, but, you know, RAI. It was an international thing, because the diocese was almost, I think, in as bad a shape as Boston was to be down the line.

In any case, when you began and spoke in about 93 languages, everybody was just stunned, like something had happened. And I remember feeling the same way. I said, "This is not just another incident in the life of the Two Bums. I'm seeing something." You took over, and the problem was not solved, of course, but at least you were able to change the vision of most of the Catholics to one of new possibilities, of a new spring for the Church. You had endless processions for every saint who ever lived, every title of the Blessed Virgin. People were overwhelmed and happy and Catholicism was being reborn.

But then, suddenly, that ends and he goes on to West Palm Beach to clean up another scandal, this one concerning the bishop himself. Two things were now running side by side: an attack on the episcopal ministry by a force seeking to tear the Church down; and on the other side, this new Church being reborn by means of what you were doing.

You eventually went to Boston, and I remember you entering the Cathedral. I thought, "My God, how does he do it?" Outside there were demonstrations from both sides—one group saying you hadn't done enough, another group saying you'd done too much—and I said, "How can you do anything like this, how can you even preach the Gospel?" But then when he went over and his homily began, he began with the phrase that I won't mention now, because it would take too long to explain. The only other person in that entire building who could have recognized that phrase was me, and I felt so moved that you would even remember. I yelled, "Oh!" and the priest next to me was astounded, and I said, "Never mind."

In any case, it was about ten minutes into the homily before you said your first English word. You took out every language in use on the Earth and greeted everybody, and finally I overheard one of the newsmen say, "You know, a new Church has been born now, it's not the same."

Tell us something about this persistent scandal, the pedophilia scandal. I think we would be wrong in ignoring that question, because it is such an important part of your life.

O'Malley: In three of the four dioceses where I have served, it has been a very important part of the ministry the Church has called me to, and one of healing. It's not been easy, but the Catholic people, I believe, have rallied around their priests and come to realize the evil and the damage that the sexual abuse of children visits upon families and communities.

Unfortunately, I think the focus is sometimes so much on the Church that people lose sight of the fact that this is a human problem, and exists outside of the Church in a way that's much more rampant. But when it involves the Church, the betrayal and the damage is magnified, and so is a very deep wound in the Body of Christ, and one that requires a sense of conversion and repentance for the full community. It is encouraging to see that the seriousness with which the Church has taken this problem seems to be helping: the incidence of sexual abuse in churches, parishes, and agencies has been greatly, greatly diminished; but still it has caused terrible harm and scandal. At the same time, whenever the Church is faced with these kinds of challenges, our God can bring good out of evil. We see how many people have rallied to support the Church. When I arrived in

Boston we had 15 seminarians, and priests were telling me, "We have to close the seminary." I said, "No, we have to keep the seminary open, and we have to invite young men to embrace the vocation." Today, we have a terrible problem: in Boston the seminary is filled, and we have to build more rooms. That's because these young men are, against the protests of their friends—and sometimes even their families—embracing a vocation because they want to help their Church. They want to be at the service of God's people, and are not frightened off by our humanity, by our sins and failings. They want to be a part of the new evangelization. It's a very moving experience to see how God's grace works in the Church. I am very edified by the faith of our people, their generosity, their desire to make the Lord's Kingdom more visible in our midst.

Albacete: One brief word about another subject that comes up when one mentions you, especially in conservative Catholic circles, and that is your decision to allow a Catholic burial for Ted Kennedy. This has been criticized as diminishing the urgency to protest the support of abortion by Catholic politicians.

O'Malley: In the case of Senator Kennedy, the position of the Church, I think, has been very clear and has not been diminished; however, the Church's mission is also to bury the dead. The burial is not just for the individual, but also for their family and the community. And so to me, it was a logical thing to be there. This is a man whose family has made great sacrifices for our country: two of his brothers were assassinated in serving our country, one them being the very first Catholic President of the United States. I think that being present at a person's funeral is not necessarily an endorsement of all of their positions, but rather a recognition of their humanity and of our need to pray for our dead.

Albacete: That's enough. I mean, that's enough. I don't want to end on that note. I think the Two Bums haven't done too bad for their first Broadway attempt. The Nuncio was just here and we request that he convey to the Holy Father our total devotion and obedience and joy at having him with us, and I'm sure he will. In any case, it's his job. But you, Cardinal O'Malley, it's not your job; you are going to be seeing him in another context, so I ask you to please mention to him that he has people here who want to be with him, who are excited, and who are determined to follow his steps and the direction in which he wants to take the Church. We are together with him in that. Please tell him that.

O'Malley: I'll be happy to tell him that the joy of the Gospel is very much alive in New York and in CL, and he'll be so glad to hear that.

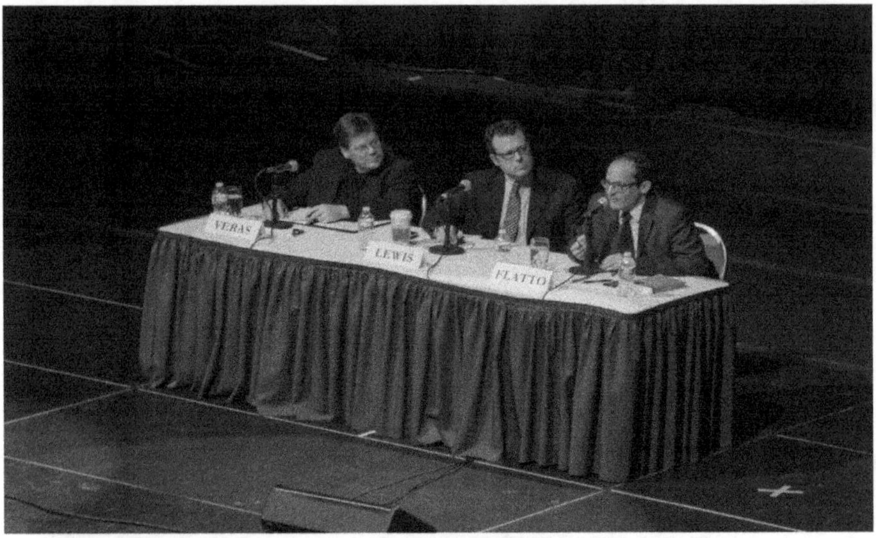

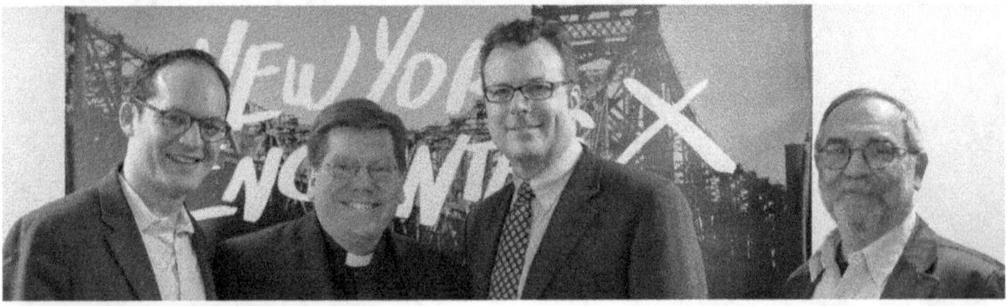

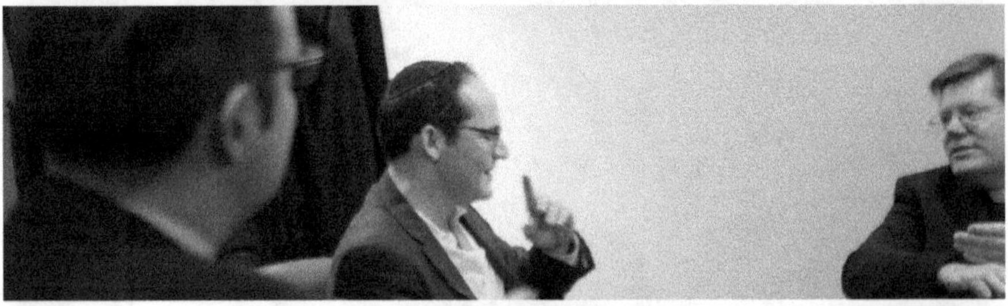

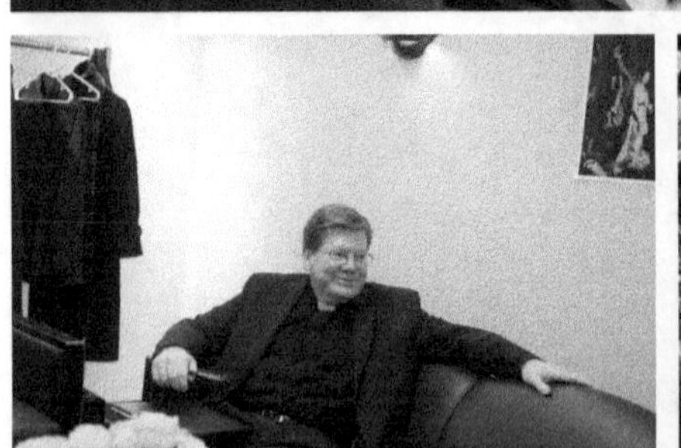

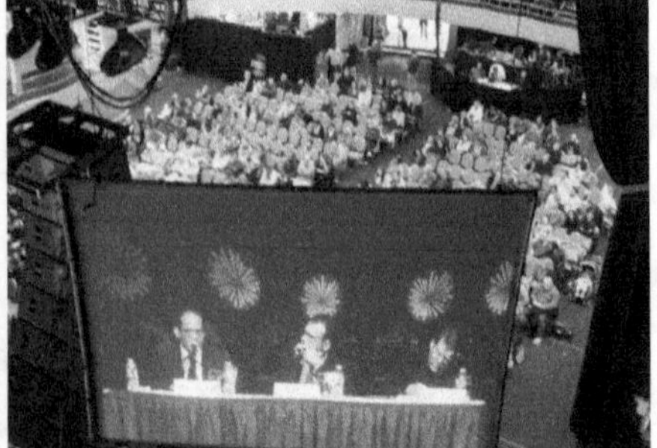

Abraham:
The Birth of the "I," the Birth of a People

Dr. David Flatto[1] and Fr. Richard Veras[2]

Introduction

We live in times when the word "belonging" often has a negative connotation: namely, diminishment or alienation of one's own individuality and freedom. Yet, in real life, we feel the need to be part of something greater that can enter into the definition of who we are, and differentiate us from others (e.g., social networking, political parties, social or religious groups). The sense of pride in "belonging" to the American people is also another undeniable fact. Why is that? Is belonging a real existential need? In the Jewish and Catholic traditions the word "belonging" is not viewed with suspicion but just the opposite: it is connected with personal salvation.

"Without Abraham, if Abraham had never been, then we would not be here now. Hebrew Psalm-writing or Hebrew prophesying, Jewish commitment or the Jewish manner of living in the world, are not like clothes on a figure, but are the origin of the figure, the figure in its origin. So that we cannot understand what the 'I' is, the 'I' who weeps, laughs, commits himself, the 'I' who lives or dies, a man cannot understand himself, nor can he love others as himself, except through God of whom he is born. Otherwise the shape of the event falls apart, blurring its sharpness. Most Christians—especially those who have studied theology—have not yet realized the value of the history of the Hebrew people for themselves. Because all the moves God makes with man pass through that history, those names: Mo-

Sunday, January 19, 2014

[1]Associate Professor of Law, Religion, and History at Penn State Law
[2]Pastor of the Church of St. Rita, New York

ses, David, Isaiah, Jeremiah […] the history of a preference, the expression of God. This is the essence of Jewish thought, and this is our first move. We cannot understand the 'I' if we do not start from Abraham. God called Abraham. What does this story teach us? That the 'I' is vocation, a choice as preference. So that, from the day of that call onwards, the 'I' is understood as an event within history. An event of dependence on God and of belonging to God. History is the 'I' revealing itself in this vocation, which becomes belonging and dependence. The 'I' is understood in time, in this relationship with God that is a history: the Covenant. Jesus is understood in the unfolding procession of men starting with Abraham, Moses, David […]. Only from within this history is the Christian conception of the 'I' and of reality developed—a revolution in the way of looking at the world."

(Luigi Giussani, Notes from a dialogue with some CL members in January 2001, published in *Traces*, February 2001)

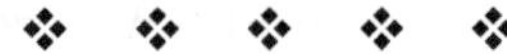

Moderator: I can't really think of a better way to start things off, and set the stage for the presentations of our two speakers on this panel, than by reading with you the passage from the book of Genesis, chapter 12:1-3, where is recounted God's calling of Abraham: "Now the Lord said to Abram, Go from your country and your kindred and your father's house to the land that I will show you. I will make of you a great nation, and I will bless you and make your name great, so that you will be a blessing. I will bless those who bless you, and the one who curses you, I will curse. And in you, all the families of the earth shall be blessed."

So, from a life lived in a familiar land, amidst familiar society, God speaks of "your country," "your kindred," and "your father's house." Abram is singled out. He is called forth to abandon his country and his father's house and to live in a new land, and in this new land something unprecedented will occur. God will not simply establish for Abram a new kindred, a new set of relatives that will replace those he left behind; no, instead, God will make of Abraham a great nation.

What exactly is meant by "a great nation"? For one thing, it seems that

Scripture suggests it is more than just a new group of kin, because it says *all* the families of the earth, *all* the groups of kin, shall be blessed in and through Abram. The calling of this man will result in a new kind of human community on the earth, created through God's blessing.

For Fr. Giussani, this call and this blessing do nothing less than reveal human identity as it is lived in the first person, both plural and singular. Who I am, who we are, is shown to us in this experience of Abraham. Fr. Giussani comments: "We cannot understand the 'I' if we do not start from Abraham. God called Abraham. What does the story teach us? That the 'I' is vocation, the choice as preference, so that from the day of that call onward the 'I' is understood as an event within history. An event of dependence on God and of belonging to God." The "I" is vocation, the entry of the person into history; and dependence and belonging are definitive of man's relation to God. The story of Abraham really promises to bring us directly to the most profound aspects of the theme for this year's NYE: "From 'I' to 'We': the Time of the Person, the Origins of a People."

Flatto: We talk about the "I"and the "We," individuals in a larger setting. On some level, in sitting here I am keenly aware of being an individual in a larger setting, coming from a different perspective. In a sense, there is a heightened individualism here, being a traditional Jew and an orthodox Jew, but there's also gratitude for larger communities of the faithful, those who adhere to a moral calling, who sense a communality. This encourages those from other backgrounds to think in a more capacious manner about what bonds us, and how in concert, together, we really have a lot of work to do to not get hermetically sealed in our own individual circumstance. If we open up and work in tandem, there are so many bridges we can build together.

So I want to thank the organizers, not just for the invite, but for the inspiration to think a little more largely. And I think, in a sense, this is a theme in my personal life, probably born of this era, in this great country, in the 21st century, where there are a lot of wonderful opportunities. There are also concomitant challenges, I would say, that go along with those opportunities. The opportunities offered frequently impel you to define yourself in a very individualistic way. We have choices, each one us, in how we want to live. This was not always the case in the past, especially in Jewish history. Jews were often minorities in larger host countries, and were forced to live in a set lifestyle. For those individual Jews wanting to break out, it was very risky, and we don't know much about those who tried, because there wasn't really a choice. But today, in 21st-century America, there is a choice in how Jewish I want to be, in how important my tradition is to me. Am I Jewish? Am I American? Am I a Westerner? Am I liberal? Am I a believer? Am I a skeptic? Am I agnostic? Am I an atheist? All of these options are all too open, in a sense, and that's daunting, too.

The great sociologist Peter Burger captured this phenomenon in his book *The Heretical Imperative*, a very worthwhile read if some out there haven't read it. In using "heretical imperative," he is returning to the Greek term *hairesis*, which means "to choose"—not in the sense of going the wrong way, but actually as an imperative, a duty to choose. Each one of us has a duty to choose, because we live in a time where choices are not so preset or predetermined. Sometimes we get lost in those choices, and sometimes we live much richer lives because of those choices. From a sociological perspective, this really captures what it is like to be religious and traditional in modern times in the West. In a very personal sense, I've had both the liberty and the opportunity—and also the challenge—of making such choices. I am part of a very traditional, Orthodox Jewish community; I am also part of a community of professionals, of lawyers; I am also an academic, I am also a real New Yorker and a Westerner. I am a lot of different things. I can't imagine really living any differently because that is the blessing of the times I live in. However, I know that it's difficult sometimes to retain a strong sense of core, purpose, and essence when you are in so many different circles. Let me just turn briefly to Abraham and then I want to deepen our understanding of Abraham through one crucial Jewish thinker; I'll get to him in just a little bit.

If you think about Abraham, he first discovers himself by breaking from a community. This is alluded to in Genesis and amplified in early Jewish commentaries on Genesis. Abraham's background is in Canaan. His father, Terah, is a quintessential idolater, a leading idolater, in the book of Joshua; rabbis have elaborated on the position of Abraham's father as an eminent idolater in Canaan. When Abraham gets the charge and the call, in Genesis 12, to leave the land of Canaan, he is told to leave his "we," to leave his community: he will only discover himself through a great individualistic march to a new land. I am sorry I keep saying Canaan—I really mean the countries of Mesopotamia. H grew up in Mesopotamia, and is supposed to leave the idolater's world. Only by breaking with the "we" he grew up with will he discover the "I."

The thinker I want to introduce is Maimonides, perhaps the greatest Jewish philosopher, a powerful medieval thinker, both philosopher and jurist, who lives in the 12th century. He lives in Spain, then ends up traveling through Israel to Egypt, where he is very aware of the surrounding cultures, both Islamic and Christian. He is of course devoted to his own Jewish tradition.

When Maimonides tells Abraham's story, he elaborates. He says, "Don't think Abraham was a kid when he left home. He actually lived a good chunk of his life in an idolater's world. If you want to understand Abraham," he says, "you need to know book one of his biography. Book one of his biography says Abraham was an idolater." He was an idolater for the first four decades of his life, and it was only through being courageous enough to break from a "we" to find an "I" who heeds the call from above, to have the courage to heed that calling, to have the inspiration to march to a new land—that Abraham discovers a true path. So sometimes the individual has to break from the "we" when the "we" restricts the individual.

Part two of the Abrahamic biography is the story we know from Genesis—Abraham in a new land. Here is the crucial point to appreciate: even though he marches solo at first, he begins to build circles, communities. He actually does not belong just to one circle. The first circle we hear about is his household. His wife, Sarah; his nephew, Volt. This is important because some of his immediate household actually continue to challenge him, they aren't all part of the same vision. Yet Abraham has a great commitment to his household. Even though he is in a new land, he understands the circle of the nuclear family. That's one circle.

Then there is the second circle, which participates in the main story of Genesis—Abraham and his offspring. In Hebrew, *Zerah Avraham*—the progeny, the seed, the followers, the faithful, those who understand the teaching of Abraham. That's the second circle. That's the one we usually pay the most attention to. And this is what all the great Abrahamic faiths focus on. What is it to follow the teaching of Abraham?

There is also a third circle, and this one is important, too: Abraham is the father of a multitude of nations. Abraham is not just focused on his nuclear family, not just focused on those who follow his teaching, but he's the father of a multitude of nations, whose blessing is projected onto a multitude of nations. Abraham, through his righteous path, knows that he can ennoble and elevate not just his nuclear household, not just those who follow the teaching, but actually a *multitude of nations*. Perhaps an entire world can ride on the shoulders of Abraham and Abraham's followers. So Abraham teaches us to think in terms of various circles. There is an individual, and then there is a collective, and the collective cannot be defined in just one uniform manner, but as different concentric circles going outward, and we have to hold all of that together.

I just want to go a drop deeper with Maimonides' teaching on Abraham. Again, Maimonides is a great 12th-century philosopher and rabbi jurist. It is so interesting how he devotes such attention to Abraham. The reason I say it's interesting is because we know a lot of the great Jewish thinkers were devoted to Moses and the Law, and in that sense Maimonides was no different. Yet Maimonides, even in his retelling of the Law, often alludes to Abraham, and he says we always have to be mindful—even in our legal, Jewish perspective—of the teachings of Abraham. So what is the core identity of Abraham? Here there is an interesting duality in Maimonides' teaching about Abraham. On the one hand, he marks Abraham as the greatest—and here I am almost in the mood to quiz the audience, those who know their Bible. I am sure there are some out there who know it well.

Actually, in Genesis, the great story of the binding of Isaac is presented as the paradigm of the one who fears or has awe of God, right? That's the story in Genesis 22. But Maimonides doesn't accent Abraham's fear or awe, drawing instead on a verse from Isaiah, where Abraham is singled out as the one who loves God. *Zarah Avraham o ravi*—in Hebrew, "to love." Abraham is the lover of God, and Maimonides stresses this. At the end of his teaching on Abraham, and also in a very crucial passage in his Code of

Law, Maimonides says the highest form of service of God is to love God. And Maimonides tells us that this requires an aspiration, it is hard to get there. Very few have achieved it. Then Maimonides draws our attention to our great father Abraham. He loved God—that's what Isaiah taught us about Abraham. So what does it mean to love God? This is deep stuff for a Sunday afternoon, so I just want to touch on Maimondean teaching about what it means to love God.

Here is the duality I want to allude to. In one place, Maimonides says what it means to love God is for the individual soul, our inners, our spiritual nature, the individual spirituality—to yearn for God and cleave to Him and His way. Of course, it begins by our aspiring to connect to God, but it is strengthened and emboldened by the reciprocal love of God for the individual. And here Maimonides goes into the great, mysterious parable of the Song of Songs. Of course, he is not the first; we know that in the Christian tradition a lot of great writers, from Origin to Clement and many more, talk about the Song of Songs as a parable of the love for God. Maimonides also develops this theme, but I want to emphasize the love of the individual soul for God. That's one aspect of loving God; it is the individual quest. But elsewhere Maimonides returns to the theme of loving God, and Abraham as the lover of God. Let me allude to a passage, and maybe later I can allude to another one, maybe two, and then I will finish my words.

In one passage he says Abraham had such great love for God that he drew other people in. Maimonides says the following: if you truly love God, then you have to share that love, because a profound love is bountiful, it spills over and is intoxicating. And of course you have to share that love with others, with your kindred spirits. I think this is broadly defined, beginning with the nuclear family, going to the community of the faithful, and then to the entire world, to spread what it means to live a noble life, a life charged with a mission of loving God. Loving God cannot be contained in the individual, but has to spill over to others. That's one teaching. And Maimonides again emphasizes: we learn this from Abraham.

Let me turn to one other context where Maimonides again refers to Abraham and says we learn a lot about loving God and the religious calling from him. He refers to the story in his Code of Law, which is an interesting context for this Genesis story.

In Genesis 18, God appears to Abraham and then three angels show up. In this passage, we almost forget about God, because Abraham busies himself with the three angels, who are messengers. He bakes bread for them, he invites them into his tent. Maimonides says that one's commitment to the love of God is reflected in one's commitment to the love of others. If you truly love God, then you love God's creatures and creations. You realize that you have to give the same loving attention to others that you would give to God. If you are so intoxicated with God that you forget about the visitor, you forget about those who need food and shelter, then there is a deficiency in your love of God. Love of God mandates turning to others.

He adds one last point in the same passage, and it's an intriguing point. I am not sure what to make of it, but let me tell you this point and then I'll take a stab at it. I'd love to hear your thoughts. Maimonides says, "How are you supposed to care for others?" Again, I think that one of the great contributions of Judaism is to break things down into detailed, concrete tasks. Maimonides says you celebrate weddings with those who are joyful; you mourn with those who are suffering loss; you give shelter to those who need a home; you give food to the hungry and you invite people in. Then Maimonides, after giving us this beautiful laundry list of ways we can focus on others, adds the following intriguing point: if you invite a guest over, that's a wonderful deed, but even more important is escorting your guests when they depart. Maimonides says that's even more important than inviting the guest in: escorting the guest out.

That, to me, is really interesting. That small teaching. I was always curious about why that is. Inviting the guest in is obvious, but why is it so important to escort the guest out? I think perhaps what Maimonides is saying is: it's one thing to create our own sacred space and to be open enough and capacious enough to invite others in; but in a sense, a higher mandate is to escort others out, to march along with others, to see where others are, their lives, their challenges. Not just to invite them into an intimate, holy, secret space, but to take that sanctity and go outwards, march with others towards where they live, in their existential realities, in their challenges, and to try to enter and bring some of the spirit and the moral calling into there, too. A lot of interesting ideas that I hope we can take away and think about. This is the balance: the individual soul loving God, but also understanding that to live it out in a full spiritual sense, there has to be a heightened awareness of our commitment and duty to others—and various circles of the others—that we have on our radar.

Veras: I trusted that Dr. Flatto would really enlighten us on Abraham, and he did, so I won't spend as much time on Abraham. I want to begin with Pope Francis' Apostolic Exhortation, *The Joy of the Gospel*, in which he has an entire section on the People of God.

We evangelize as a people, and in that section he asks, What is the Church? The Church is a mystery rooted in the Trinity, which exists concretely in the history of a people. So its root is the Trinity and its expression is a people. I don't want to get too heavy theologically, but it is really important for us as Catholics, as Christians, to contemplate the Trinity. What does the Trinity tell us? God has never been alone. *Alone* has never existed. It simply has never existed. The foundation of all reality is a people: Father, Son, and Holy Spirit—a mysterious community of persons, each one Himself, and this impossible unity is completely one. The root of everything, then, is communion. If we are created in God's image, it means that "completely alone" is a lie. We tend to think of ourselves as solely individual, and that we add on a community later, as something extra. But no, we are made for communion. To act as if we don't belong in a communion is to take on a lie. Communion generates us: existentially, profoundly, ontologically. Loneliness is a distortion, we become degenerated.

This is expressed in human experience. Any teacher, from kindergarten to 12th grade, if a student is extremely difficult in class, having problems, what is the first thing they think? There are problems in the family, or problems in the place where this child belongs, because a lack of belonging immediately expresses itself in an unrest, in a degeneration. What is the worst possible punishment for a prisoner? Solitary confinement. Because we are not made to be alone. In revelation, again, God tells Abraham to leave his kindred, not to be alone, but to be with Him. It is almost as if God was escorting Abraham out, marching with Abraham. And He promises

Abraham a nation, a people.

In early Christianity, the earliest Fathers of the Church looked at those three angels in Genesis 18 as the first manifestation of a Trinity. God appears to Abraham, and these are three angels, three visages of God. In Rublev's famous icon of the visitors, of the Trinity, the three of them are around the table and there is an empty space. Because we are invited in. God invites Abraham, and through Abraham He invites a chosen people, the people of Abraham. But, as Christians, we believe that God in His mercy becomes flesh in Jesus Christ to invite the rest of us, to invite all of us, to invite an entire nation. Therefore I want to look at Jesus. The first thing they noticed about Jesus in the Gospel of Mark is that He spoke with authority. This one speaks with an authority they had never seen before. Why? Because, for Jesus, He is not talking about a God he knows of; He doesn't know *about* God, he *knows God*: God as Father. He experienced Himself, as we heard yesterday with David Schindler, as the eternal Son, this eternal belonging. So His confidence, His certainty, was always His certainty in belonging. He was fully human, fully an "I" generated by a "We" forever, since before we or the earth existed. He was so attractive as a person, an individual, because he was always aware of His belonging. Jesus doesn't do a single miracle, doesn't preach a single sermon, doesn't heal a single blind person or lame person, doesn't do any of these things until the baptism by John the Baptist, until the Voice says, "You are my beloved Son, in You I am well-pleased." He does nothing until that is manifested and heard by others, so it is clear. Jesus will say later,"I only do what I see the Father doing." Everything good, all the love, the authority, all of Jesus' ability to embrace—because "I know I belong to the Father; I and the Father are one."

What does Jesus do? He forms a people. Very shortly after the baptism, he forms a people: the apostles, Mary Magdalene, Mary, Martha, and Lazarus. A people is formed. When people were taken by Christ, it was so interesting because, reminiscent of what we've just heard, when I belong to Christ, I see myself belonging to those who belong to Him. That dinner with the fishermen, when He calls Mathew—fishermen and tax collectors, this impossible unity. The tax collectors, those who perhaps had decided that they do not belong, they'd removed themselves from belonging—Jesus goes right up and calls the tax collectors just as he called the fishermen. There was this dinner, and it had to be a huge choice of the fishermen to remain. They don't just remain, they don't just tolerate each other. As time goes by, they love each other. They become one as a community. Jesus will pray for them at the Last Supper. "I have given them the glory that You gave me, Father, so that they may be one as we are one." The Church: rooted in the Trinity, as Pope Francis says, and expressed in the history of a people.

In the same discourse, when Jesus prays that they all may be one, He promises the Spirit. The third person of the Trinity. How will you be made one? The Spirit will come. The apostles say, How can You leave us? With You we rediscovered who we are, never meant to be alone, meant to be looked at with Your gaze. And Jesus promises, I am not leaving you, I will send the Spirit. Saint Augustine says the Spirit is the love between the Father and the Son. He is the togetherness, the unity, if you will. Saint Paul was persecuting Christians: when Jesus appeared to Paul, He said, "Why are you persecuting Me?" Not *them*, but *Me*. "I pray for them that they be one as we are one." "Why, Paul, are you persecuting Me?" "Who are you, sir?" Singular. "I am Jesus, whom you are persecuting." Paul had never met Jesus in the flesh like Peter, James, John, and the apostles did. Jesus, when asked, "Who are you?"spoke for the unity of Christians, the Church: "I am Jesus, whom you are persecuting." And how does Paul remain in relationship with Christ? Jesus said to him, "Go on the straight street, be baptized by Ananias." You want to stay with me, Paul? You will stay with me. You stay with the members of my body, you stay with the Church.

You see? Paul never went preaching alone. He always had a companion. Barnabas, Silas, Luke, Mark—the Gospel writers were his companions at certain points. When Paul was in prison, he always asked for visitors. At the end of Paul's letters there are greetings, there is a list full of names. Because Paul says we are the Mystical Body of Christ, this mysterious unity. There is a beautiful scene in Acts Chapter 20 where Paul is leaving Ephesus and the presbyters in Ephesus are weeping. They are embracing him and weeping, because Paul is the source of their unity. Why? Because Paul understood "I am not alone. I carry with me the companionship of God, the companionship of the Church." Paul generates a people, just as Jesus did. As Christ belongs to the Father, He is attractive. Paul was so aware of his belonging to Christ that he became completely attractive.

I don't want to take too much time, but he says in one letter, basically, I know what you all say about me: my letters are great; but when I show up I don't look so impressive. So pay attention to the letters, he says. But the presbyters of Ephesus paid attention to Paul and came to love him, to really love him. Paul had a great awareness of his belonging. And perhaps with us in an individualistic, secular society, we are less aware of this ontological belonging, this belonging that goes to the root of reality, our belonging to the God who made us, the God who makes us.

It is interesting that in the book of Deuteronomy, when God is correcting His people at one point, He says, Since you have provoked me with a no-God, I will provoke you with a no-people. No God, no people. Because our belonging is deeper. A superficial belonging is not enough to create a people. When our belongings tend to be superficial, they are conditional. You belong *until*. But it is beautiful, isn't it, that visit of the angels to Sarah, when they prophesied that she would have a child within in a year. She laughed, and one of the angels said, "Why did you laugh?" And she said, "I didn't laugh." He said, "Yes, you did," and off they go. This is one of the most important moments in salvation history. God kept Sarah in mind, and she had a son.

Sarah's belonging was deeper than her immorality, if you will. And Sarah said, I have reason to laugh now and everyone will laugh with me. Because who is this God? He is not separate, He calls us, we belong. Peter denies Christ three times and Jesus says, "Do you love me?" You still belong. The thief on the cross, "Lord remember me." "Today you are with Me in paradise, you are with Me." This belonging is deeper even than sin. This belonging is always renewable, it is objective. I can dishonor my parents if I want, but I look like my dad, I talk like him, and I have the fair skin of my mom. I can travel all over the world, and I still am going to look like him. This is belonging to the Trinity.

A couple of pastoral examples, because certainly the more aware I am of this belonging, the more I am built up as a person. The more I am certain of myself, like Christ, the more I carry within me this communion. If there is lack of awareness, it is less visible, but this communion is still there.

As a pastor, there is a day of the year as fascinating as it is annoying, especially for priests. Ash Wednesday is amazing. Because on Ash Wednesday every Catholic wants ashes. And so priests in our parishes, they are marked men on Ash Wednesday. When I finish, I escape into the rectory. I don't go to the parking lot or the office because someone is going to catch me. In Saint Patrick's Cathedral, there are lines out the door. Forget service of the Word or Mass. The seminaries are empty because the seminarians are sent to help. Everybody shows up wanting ashes. I may not believe in the teachings of the Church, I might not live according to the Church, I might only enter the door of the church on Ash Wednesday, but somehow there is a sense that not getting ashes is going over a line I don't want to go over. And not only am I going to church, I am walking around the rest of the day with ashes on my forehead. I am announcing to the world, "Yes, that's me." And I don't know what level of awareness this is. Are they saying, "I am a sinner?" Are they saying, "I belong?" There is a sense of the People of God, there is a belonging that I want to assent to on some level, that I want to witness to. And so Ash Wednesday is fascinating. It is the ideal? No. I want to be more aware.

In my parish, St. Rita in Staten Island, about a third of our parishioners are Indians, some of whom will call themselves Thomas' Christians because they were evangelized by St. Thomas. They have an affection for St. Thomas, who went a place that must have been so strange to him. But I see today in my parish, every Sunday, at daily Mass, I see the people that Thomas built. When Thomas went, how aware he must have been: I belong, I belong to that Man. I doubted, I refused to believe my brother apostles when they said He was risen, I doubted Him by doubting the Church, by doubting the apostles. And still I belong. The awareness of St. Thomas in the history of the Church, the awareness of the founders of religious orders and lay movements, St. Francis, St. Ignatius, Mother Teresa. We understand her first followers were high school students, so attractive was this woman! Fr. Giussani, too. These people had such a sense of belonging, and such a way of looking at others, that it told the others that you belong. What so many of them have in common is that they didn't plan to found anything. They lived their lives, they joyfully lived their belonging.

Inadvertently, unknown to them, surprisingly to them, they were attractive to others. They didn't even realize that their being was an invitation, like the icon of the Trinity. That their being seemed to say to people, "Follow me, come with me, stay with me." We see how the awareness of this belonging can build us up. But no matter how ignorant we are, or how dim our awareness, it can be taken up like that. We can be reminded of it like that.

What does Fr. Giussani say about this belonging? That it has two characteristics. One, it is all-embracing. The awareness of my belonging determines all my relationships, the way I look at everything in reality. Two, it is catholic, it is universal. It is a companionship open to all who encounter it, a signal to affirm the truth in everything, that we become protagonists, ready to welcome everything because every aspect of reality arises from Him, arises from God.

I want to begin my conclusion with a quote from Pope Francis' *The Joy of the Gospel,* in he speaks about how Christianity generates a people, how the presence of God among us generates a people. It generated first of all the Chosen People, and then through Jesus Christ it generates the nations. Pope Francis writes that countless peoples have received the grace of faith, which has been brought to flower in their daily lives and handed on in a language of their own culture. The history of the Church shows that Christianity does not have just one cultural expression, but rather it reflects the different faces of cultures and peoples in which it is received. And in the diversity of peoples who experience the gift of God, the Church shows forth the beauty of God in her varied faces. The Church takes up the values of different cultures and becomes the bride bedecked with her jewels. The variety of peoples in the expression of Christianity are the jewels bedecking the bride. The Church, the bride of Christ.

I am very blessed at St. Rita's, because when Christmas comes we have our school celebration of Christmas, we have the Indian celebration of Christmas with Mass and a party in the gym, we have the Sri-Lankan celebration with Mass and a party in the gym, and we have the Filipino celebration. It is very difficult for us to find a day leading up to Christmas to get all the space we need for all the different expressions of the peoples. But a bride is bedecked with her jewels. And what is the image the Jesus gives of the Church? We see it in Revelation: the Church as the bride of Christ. When a man marries a woman, a human being marries a human being; you can only marry one who is like you. So we can only be the bride of Christ if it is possible that God becomes one with us.

In the Church we have the communion of saints. We are a communion of peoples—Christ generates a people. St. Thomas was one of the members of that people, but Thomas goes as a fulfilled person who knows his belonging, and he generates a people in India. A person generates people, and from those peoples we get persons, who then go and generate peoples again, and from there you get persons. This is a spilling over, an overflowing of God's love. All of reality is the overflowing of the love of the Trinity. It is unimaginable, this never-ending generating of people. Those who generate are generated by those they generate.

There is a beautiful story of a man from Africa who came to visit Fr. Giussani. He said to Fr. Giussani, "You are my father." And Fr. Giussani said to him, "No, you are my father." When I heard that story, it really bothered me and I thought, What does it mean? Because how generated Giussani must have been. I never met you before. You are generated by me? That means that within our faces, within our people God is active, so you who are generated by me are my father, because I am generated by what God is doing among the people of God. This unimaginable unity that we yearn for does not fulfill, however. Pope Francis once said we are not fulfilled, we are on a pilgrimage. This is the ideal. Ultimately, heaven is a wedding feast. But we know that weddings don't come from nowhere. You don't walk into a church and marry a stranger. So the fulfillment of this unity is at the end; the courtship is now, we savor a taste of this unity now. I see it in the peoples in my parish. I became a priest because of Communion and Liberation, the reality that generates the New York Encounter. The promise is in the flesh *now*. The claim of the Church, the unimaginable claim, is "I am Jesus, I am Jesus among you." "Father, may they be one as we are one. Not, May it be added onto what they already are, no; Father, may they become aware of who they are. May they become aware of this profound, ontological belonging that carries within it such a promise, such an expectation."

Moderator: I'll turn to Dr. Flatto. I was very struck by the way you characterized these concentric circles, the way in which anyone who truly loves God is always both amongst those who are following Abraham, and also welcoming and accompanying the other in the journey the other is taking. There are a few universalities here. Can you tell us a little bit more about how you see this call to universal human brotherhood? And how it relates to other views of universalities that we have today?

Flatto: Thank you for the interesting follow-up question. This is a tough challenge,to give a Jewish perspective on large questions, and obviously there are a lot of different perspectives. A Jewish perspective is never a perspective, it is perspectives, right? There are debates on everything. I think here, too, we can find such a range of viewpoints: those who focus more on one of the circles, if you will, and those who are mindful that there are a variety of circles. To me, the latter perspective is the perspective within Judaism that I feel challenged and inspired by, and that's what I think is very timely to share. We live in an era in which we are greatly imperiled if we just focus inwardly. There is a great chance that if we draw boundaries and just look inside of our post-provincial community, we will be marginalized in ways that are unfortunate and not worth the price. I don't think that needs to be the strategy. That's why I return to great teachings of Abraham, the great teachings of Maimonides, of some of the great models for us of the religious calling. And I think that the religious calling really invites us to *think*: both in terms of deep, profound commitment to our nuclear family, our faith community, the faithful—and, more largely, with those whose moral values we share, and then humanity. I really think we have to constantly be involved in this challenging, coordinated participation in various communities.

I am tempted to give more teachings of Maimonides on this. Let me just allude to one teaching of his that I think is relevant. It is really striking that Maimonides opens his Code of Law—I just want to emphasize how much he wrote, okay? He wrote two really eternal works that 800 years later we sit and pour over. One is his Code of Law, which is focused on the minutia of Jewish law, and the other is his philosophical work, probably a little bit more familiar to some here, *The Guide for the Perplexed*. One interesting citation from his Code of Law, which is full of detail in explaining how to observe the traditional Jewish Sabbath, asks: if there is an accident, how do you compensate, how do you go to a ritual bath for purification? Lots of details, you see. Yet in his Code of Law, it is really fascinating that in the first chapters, Maimonides speaks in general terms about having a relationship with God, about appreciating the wonder of creation, about studying science and physics, and then contemplating the profound ideas of metaphysics.

There is actually a word that is almost missing from the first four chapters. Maimonides hardly ever refers to Israel or the Jews. And this is because Maimonides deliberately opens his Code to humanity. All of humanity has a moral mission, has a duty to have a relationship with God. So he opens his Code that way, the first four chapters, and the way I know this is a correct inference is that he also closes his Code with a description of the Messianic era in universal terms. Maimonides says we should begin with a universal focus. Only in Chapter 5 does he talk about Israel and the normative duties of Israel. And here, too, he says that the individual in Israel who is committed to the moral life, the spiritual life, the normative life, the life of great rigor and great duties, great commandments—always has to balance his or her individual responsibility with an awareness of the community, i.e., the universal humanity of which they are a part. So, even when he introduces a normative charge to Israel, her duties, her commandments, immediately he corrects course and says don't get entrapped in a too-provincial way of thinking and living. In other words, your calling is a heightened responsibility, your job is even more ambitious. You are part of many circles, don't neglect any one of them. Always be mindful of all of that.

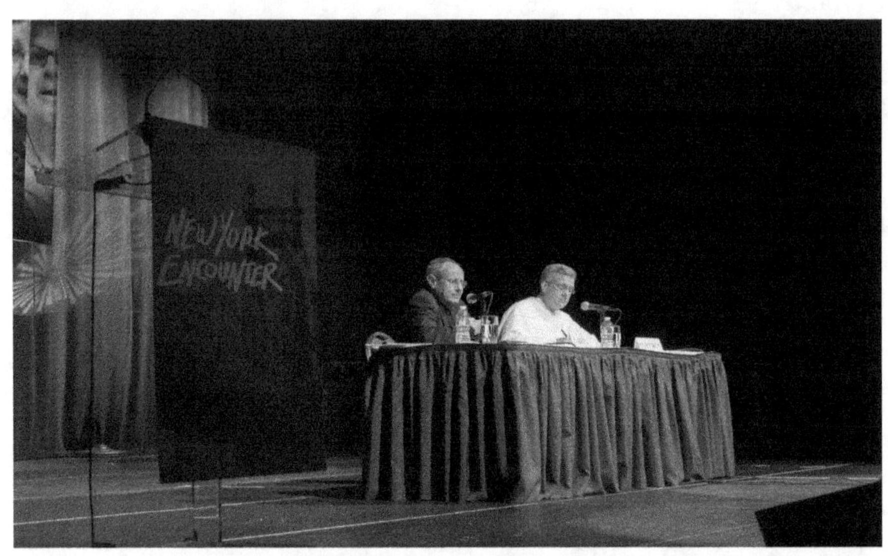
NEW YORK
ENCOUNTER

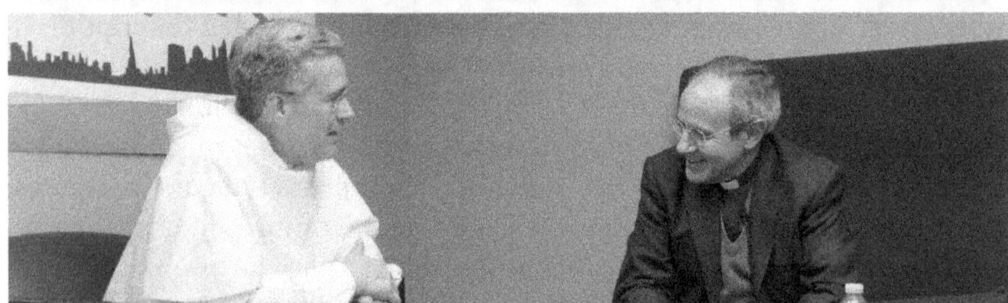

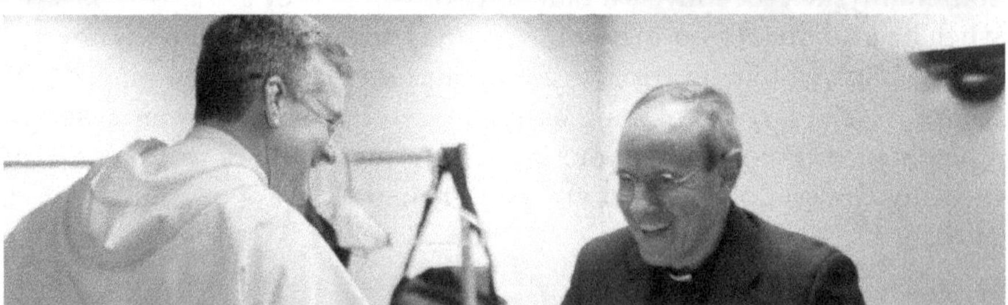

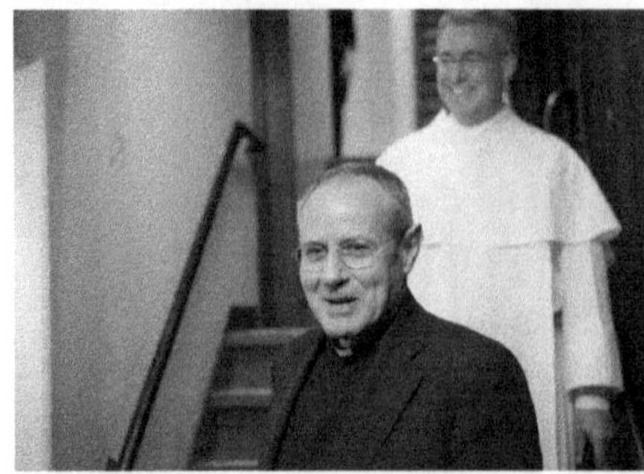

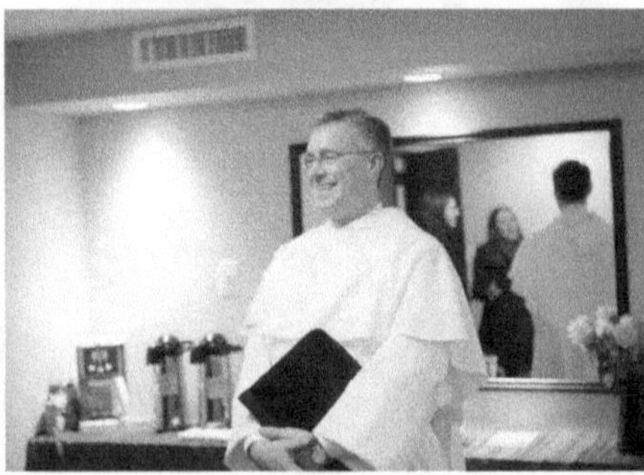

From "I" to "We": The Time of the Person, The Origins of a People

Fr. Peter John Cameron[1] and Fr. Julián Carrón[2]

Introduction

What is the person? Who are we, really? What can allow the person to "happen," and last, in all of his or her full stature?

"It is impossible to believe on our own. Faith is not simply an individual decision which takes place in the depths of the believer's heart, nor a completely private relationship between the 'I' of the believer and the divine 'Thou,' between an autonomous subject and God. By its very nature, faith is open to the 'We' of the Church; it always takes place within her communion."

(Pope Francis, *Lumen Fidei*)

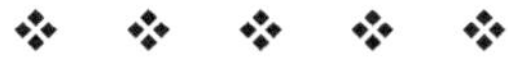

Cameron: All of us have come together in this room because something has moved us. So the experience that we all share, sitting in these chairs, is that we're looking for something, we're looking for something more. And what we want to know is: What does the Christian faith have to offer our life right now that is truly relevant? We don't want life to be a ritual. We all want to meet Jesus Christ. We've met Jesus Christ, but we want to know Him more closely, more intimately. We want His life to be our life. And

---

Sunday, January 19, 2014

[1]Editor-in-Chief, *Magnificat*

[2]President of the Fraternity of Communion and Liberation

the sadness that we feel in our life when that's not the case can make us feel like failures. Even more, we want our life to change. We want to be like Zacchaeus in the Gospel. We wonder, and something moves us, tells us that the greatness we see in the people of the Gospels is possible for us. So I guess that's our question: Is it possible for us to actually live the greatness of the people in the Gospels before we get to heaven? We know heaven's going to be great, but do we have to wait until then for this greatness to happen? That's our problem. We are hoping you will help us, and maybe we can start by framing the problem with this question: What exactly is the role of the Christian event in life?

Carrón: I thank you, Fr. Cameron, for this question, because yesterday morning I was struck by a comment, similar to this question, raised by a university student in a meeting. The comment was, "My desire is to not miss out on anything, like the beautiful things." I think that this way of expressing the longing we have, every one of us, is beautiful. We decide not to miss out on every beautiful thing that happens along the way of our life. Who of us wouldn't agree with this student? Everyone's desire is to not miss out on any beautiful thing that happens in life.

In front of a statement like his, each one of us has to decide whether to take it seriously or to forget it. This is the first decision that each one of us has to make every morning, every moment of life, to take seriously this urgency, this human longing. If a person takes this question seriously, then all of a sudden life becomes full of intensity, of curiosity, full of this urgency to find an adequate answer to this kind of question. This may seem unimportant, but if we don't have this longing for something, then everything in life becomes flat, without interest, because in essence we await nothing: we wake up in the morning with an expectation of nothing. What is our interest in waking every morning? If we take seriously a question like this, then waking each morning, going to work or to study, meeting people or reading a book—every moment becomes a possibility for seeking an answer to this question, of learning how to not miss out on the beautiful things which happen. It generates a curiosity in us, an attention to every hint that reality can offer us in response to this question. We start to live everything with a desire to not miss out on any beautiful thing. This inner desire becomes the criterion or judgment because it contains the possibility of making a comparison between our hearts and what we can find in every human experience. All of a sudden, relationships become not a burden to bear, but a possibility of finding something in others' experience that can be useful in answering my question. Everything is full of promise, full of a promise that each one of us can discover in every circumstance.

But, when we are really careful and attentive to every experience of people we meet, not every experience has the capacity to answer these desires, because many people don't know how to not miss out on the beautiful things that happen in life. Not every experience has the same interest, the same value. The goal, then, is to wake every morning and live every instant with this curiosity. This is to live life as a human being who coincides with his own nature, with his own desire, with his own longing for something that makes life really worthwhile.

If we observe what happened to John and Andrew at the beginning of the Gospel, we see that this is how they lived. These are two people who woke that morning longing for something. They had heard about somebody called John the Baptist; they were curious and went to meet him. And in that moment, something happened that changed their lives forever.

I was struck by the Pope's recent preaching on the final feast of the Christmas season, because I think it can offer an answer to this question that we are talking about. It was the Feast of the Epiphany, and the Pope said this feast lets us see a double movement: in one direction, the movement of God towards the world, towards humanity; and in the other direction, the movement of men towards God. Let us think of religion as the quest for truth, the journey of the nation towards peace, interior peace, justice and freedom, because we desire all of these, they are part of our heart. This movement of each one of us has been answered by another movement, that of God towards us to meet this movement of our heart and answer this longing for happiness, for justice, for freedom. And this double movement, said the Pope, is driven by a mutual attraction. What is it that draws God? It is love for us. We are his children and he loves us. He wants to free us from evil, from sickness, from death, from burden—because a life without interest is really boring—to bring us to His home, to His kingdom. Jesus is the meeting point of this mutual attraction. This is the meaning of the

Christian event. Jesus is the meeting point of this mutual attraction, this double movement of God and of us. He is God among men. He is God *among*. But who took the initiative? God, always. God's love always comes before our own. He, seeing this longing for Him, for a happiness we are incapable of giving ourselves, by our projects, by our attempts—God has had pity on us and has moved towards us to satisfy our longing for fulfillment. He always takes the initiative. He waits for us. He invites us. The initiative is always his.

This is something that Pope Francis emphasizes every time he speaks to us: this initiative of Christ towards us, this first movement, this love that is at the beginning, the starting point of this movement towards our loneliness, our boredom, our incapacity to not miss out on the beautiful things in life: this is the impact of the Christian event on life. It's an experience that we can see in John and Andrew's encounter with Jesus. They encountered Jesus, then someone encountered John and Andrew; then someone encountered those who had encountered John and Andrew, and on and on, until this event has arrived to us through somebody in which we can see a possibility of living life in such a way that we can't miss out on every beautiful thing that happens. Every one of us has this desire to meet someone like Him, someone we can recognize now, whose presence can save everything we want saved, and keep everything we want kept—forever. All the beautiful relationships that happen in our life, all the beautiful things that we want to keep with us forever—it's impossible for us to maintain this desire in all His freshness, in all His beauty. We need the help of someone greater, someone in whom this desire can really be fulfilled.

Cameron: I would say the Magi are very much like the student you mentioned. They had this longing, they had this urgency, they were driven by it. They woke up in the morning, they were going to their job, really looking for something more. Then one day they looked into the sky and saw this beautiful star, which is kind of an event, and they decided to pack their bags, kiss their wives goodbye, gas up the camels and head east—or west, I guess; they were east. So, this longing, this urgency that you are talking about, this is not just for Christians, then. It's for every human being.

Carrón: It's for every human being. Because each one of us can look at himself or herself and discover if this longing is his or hers. Who doesn't desire to have the possibility of keeping the most important things that happen in life? For instance, if someone loves another—who doesn't desire to keep this love alive forever? We want these beautiful things to remain alive always. We don't want them to only be something that happens in a given moment and after a while fades away, disappears as a present experience and remains only as a remembrance. No, we want them to be a present event that involves all our lives. We are really lucky when somebody offers us a job: we start the job with all our energy, all our curiosity, all our desire to make a real contribution to the company; but, after a while, the normal difficulties and our incapacity for living another way make working something boring or difficult to bear. What happens? The starting point is this curiosity, this desire for going to work, this possibility of fulfillment, but after a while everything changes and the promise can't be fulfilled. This is the origin of a movement that brings us little by little to a skepticism.

Cameron: And that is part of our problem. We feel like happiness is an illusion, that we've been deceived into thinking that there is this fulfillment. But as you say, the event that we are looking for is not something of our own making, it's not of our own initiative. It begins in a love and it has to be great enough to take up all of that urgent longing, all of that desire. But why, Fr. Carrón, is it so important to speak about Christianity as an event? What's the significance of that word?

Carrón: I think it's important to look at this question, because many times we speak of Christianity not as an event but as some kind of doctrine or ethics, or things to do or feelings to cultivate. After a while, however, none of these things can resist the challenges of life. What is important is that we can talk of an *event*. What is the importance of an event?

The best way to understand this kind of thing is to look to our own experience, because in our experience we can find the light to understand this kind of question. The first thing is to look for a significant event in our own life, to accept what happens when a significant event happens in our life. The most common event in which we can see the relevance an event has in our own life is falling in love. Let's look at this fact together. If we are attentive to this fact we can acknowledge some signs, details, and repercussions in our own lives. The first of these is that this event introduces a new way of dealing with ordinary things. When somebody is in love, he doesn't change jobs or lose the difficulties and challenges he has to face in daily life. Everything remains as before, but something new is happening in his way of dealing with the challenges of daily life: relationships, jobs, circumstances. This newness is so evident in someone who is in love that people around us can't help but realize this newness, and many times someone asks us, "Are you in love?" They don't know anything about what is happening in us, but they identify this kind of newness with an event that happened in our life.

This means that an event is the possibility of introducing something really new in the way we can live ordinary life. We can recognize whether an event has become the criterion of our living by its influence on our way of living. An event introduces a newness that no other strategy or effort or attempt has been able to introduce. This is not a decision we make to do ordinary things in a new way; it's a surprise. We are surprised by this newness in the way we can deal with things, the ordinary things that we need to face. Sometimes I become aware of this newness through others, because they made me aware of what is really happening. We are expecting something to introduce this newness because no other attempt has been able to do it. Therefore, this is the only possibility we can figure out, that really can change our daily life into a life full of meaning, full of intensity, full of warmth and tenderness, full of all we need to live life as a human being, according to our desires.

Cameron: So this is what Pope Benedict XVI means, then, in *Deus Caritas Est*, when he says being Christian is not the result of an ethical choice or a lofty idea, but the encounter with an event, a person which leads to a new horizon and a decisive direction. And that's what you would call this newness.

Carrón: This is, I think, a summary of what we are talking about, because Pope Benedict identified in a precise way what is the point. It's not an effort made by us, it is not a strategy, it is not some kind of idea that came to our minds. It is an event. We don't know how to deal with the important challenges of daily life. We are unable to answer these kinds of questions by ourselves, and for this reason we are looking for an event, and this is only the first step. As a second point, experience convinces us that only when this event happens is there the possibility of a real newness in our lives. The Christian event is a symbol, the most important symbol of this method that Pope Benedict spoke about.

Cameron: And we want to talk about this newness, but before we move on to that question: just to clarify, because I think sometimes the notion of "event" can become a little abstract for people, and we think about "event" as, I don't know, a very special occasion like a 50th birthday party or something like that; but what you're saying is, an event is a person. So as you said, just meeting somebody can make this newness happen. I think that has been the experience of many, if not all, of us here at the New York Encounter. We come here not looking for ideas, because there are a lot of places to get ideas; but we come here because we want to meet persons, we want to be face to face with persons, to be in the presence of persons with the hope that somehow that newness will take hold of us. And I know that, in the few hours I've been here, it has.

Carrón: Otherwise, what is the meaning of being here today?

Cameron: Fr. Carrón, what newness does this event bring to life? And, in answering the question, if you could help us see it in a Gospel example, so that we can understand it very concretely.

Carrón: I am very happy to read for you a text from Giussani, in which he demonstrates, from the Gospel, the repercussion of this event in the life of a person who has met Christ.

"Jesus is there, speaking at the door of a house, and all the people are blocking the passageway to hear him talk. At noon He had to eat, but as the Gospels say, He didn't forget to eat. It was as if, in front of people who were suffering, He couldn't go away. Two fellows arrived with a stretcher, carrying a paralytic. He was smaller than others his age and said, 'Let us by, coming through, excuse us,' the way ambulances use sirens when traffic is blocked, but nobody lets them pass until police arrive. 'Let us by,' but the people still did not move, remaining in their places to listen to Jesus.

Then those two fellows, clever guys, go behind the house. See, the houses were only one storey and normally had a roof made of mud and stone. They hauled him up to the roof, broke a bit of the roofing material, and lowered him behind Christ. Christ turned, fixed His gaze on him and said, 'Take heart, your sins are forgiven.' With His great acumen, Jesus sensed the depression and moral weakness which normally accompanies long illness. The man had been paralyzed for 30 years, and this is an observation which is quite true psychologically. Afterwards, He heals him as a challenge to the Pharisees who were there in front, scandalized because He'd said, 'Take heart, your sins are forgiven.' But imagine that fellow getting up from his bed. Imagine that paralytic finding himself free, standing, who is there among people like everyone else. Everyone looks at him with curiosity, a bit frightened because of the strange, supernatural fact that happened in their midst. Then that man will follow Him, will understand many things that he said.

"In any case, the main thing was comprehensible to everyone. He said He was the Messiah. What happened afterwards to this man who'd been healed? Imagine his relationship with God now, the way he would pray that evening, the way he would go to the temple next time, the sentiments he had when he saw the sun set or rise. The next day he went to work with his soul overflowing with gratitude for the forgiveness. And his soul overflowed with a mysterious awe, an awe that the mystery of God could reach all the way to him through that Man who had healed him."

In short, the sentiment towards Jesus, the way he said, *Jesus*, the way he went with the others to the village to announce the Kingdom of God, to become friends, the way he thought about his past life, the way he had treated his family members, the way he treated them now, were all actions that started from a consciousness of himself, from a sense of his person, from a physiognomy that was shaped by this event. It is impossible that something like this happens in the life of a person and doesn't shape his way of dealing with reality. This is an event that builds my own "I." I am the same as yesterday, but different, and when someone meets one like him it's impossible not to recognize that something has happened to them. "What's happening to you? What has happened to you?" And this is the possibility of touching Christ as an event, not as a preaching, not as a doctrine, not as ethics, but in teaching a human being the way of seeing the totality of things. Ordinary things—the sunset, or waking in the morning, or going to a job, or meeting people—everything is determined by this event. Nothing else, no other theory, doctrine, or ethics can change life like an event such as this. And all this newness is not a result of a decision. I am determined, I am shaped by an event like this that changed my life. This is Christianity. Not something that I learned and afterwards need to apply. It's the newness the encounter with Christ introduces into my life. It's another thing. Christianity is another thing, something other than what we have in mind. It's something like this. It's this event, which has been brought to me through a human being, with all the limits, with all the difficulties, even the sins, but with a newness, with the capacity for fascination, a capacity for attraction that I've never had before in life.

And life is better this way. It's better to live life with this intensity, this capacity for loving everything, this capacity for coinciding with myself in everything I have to do. Instead of waiting to start living, we have the possibility of living this newness in every moment of our life.

Cameron: This is amazing. If you are talking about the paralytic in the Gospel, the newness is not simply that now he can move, stand up, and walk, but it's all these other things: it's freedom in the way he looks at his past; it's the wonder he has before beauty; it's the sort of tenderness he has towards everything he has to do, even when he has to go to work; it's the way he thinks about his past life and his sins and the way he thinks about others. And there are many examples of this from the Gospel. I think of the parable of the prodigal son because, again, he was moved out of this terrible place because of the event of a person, a father—you know, he goes back to his father. What many people don't know about the prodigal son is that when he got home he married the woman at the well. That's one of the marks of newness. But Fr. Carrón: this is all very interesting, yes, but these are all people in the past. This event can't happen to us today, can it?

Carron: This is a good question, because it's the question that my student, when I was teaching high school, put before me: the Gospels are full of beautiful things, beautiful and miraculous things, but they don't happen anymore. This is the challenge of an historical event. It's not enough that this event can happen in the past: it must be possible for us to share in it, to participate in an event like this. It must be possible in the present. This is the real challenge that Christianity has in front of humanity today, to show that this is not only preaching, or ethics, or feelings, but something that has happened in the present. Witnesses of this event can show that this happens even now, and in fact keeps happening in the present.

I want to tell you something recounted by our friend Savorana in his biography of Fr. Giussani. He tells us of the moment his life changed in such a way that, from this moment on, nothing for him was ever really the same. It was the moment in which a teacher introduced the first chapter of the Gospel of St. John. Giussani was fond of an Italian poet, Leopardi, because in the man's poems he recognized something of the longing for happiness that he felt in his own heart. So, when he was 15 years old, he devoted part of his time to learning by heart all the poems of Leopardi, in which the poet expresses in a beautiful way the drama of this longing for happiness. This always strikes me when reading Giussani: somebody who was 15 years old could not find another companion for living except a poet. That he recognizes his longing for happiness is simply amazing. This is a testimony to the humanity of Giussani. Because it's crucial to understand the repercussion of this moment in which a teacher introduces the Gospel of St. John. The class was full of people in this moment, the seminary was full of people, and the classes were very, very large. Many of Giussani's classmates heard the same Gospel but it didn't have the same repercussion. It's amazing. Because only if we are longing for something can we intercept the answer. And because of this, Giussani called that day a beautiful day: "Everything happened for me like the surprise of a beautiful day, when my tenth-grade teacher—I was 15—read and then explained the first page of the Gospel of St. John. At that time it was mandatory to read that piece at the end of every mass." You remember because you are a little old.

Cameron: Thank you for reminding me.

Carrón: I was little.

Cameron: I get discounts at Dunkin' Donuts, though.

Carrón: I had heard this Gospel thousands of times and nothing happened. But this day, the beautiful day, came when my teacher explained the Word of God, that is, the Word in which everything consists was made flesh. Many of us have heard this Word many times, many times without anything happening. But for him it was the moment in which everything changed.

Fr. Giussani's insistence on "the Word was made flesh," that beauty was made flesh, goodness was made flesh—love, life, truth was made flesh—does not exist in our platonic, super-celestial world. The Word was made flesh and is one among us. In that moment, Giussani remembered Leopardi's poem "To His Lady." In that moment, he saw all of Leopardi's begging as a crying out for something 1,800 years after the fact, after the event. It had already happened, and St. John had announced that the Word was made flesh.

But what was the repercussion of this event in Giussani's life? Initially, only a sentimental one. Nothing happened. Going back to this incident 60 years later, Giussani says, "I was a young seminarian. An obedient, exemplary boy, and nothing happened. But one day something really happened that radically changed my life." In that moment his life was invested by the event as a persistent memory that assailed his thought, and provoked him to re-evaluate the daily banality. From that moment on, the instant was no longer trivial for him. The instant: the importance of the instant, of every instant, is significant for him. Everything that was beautiful, true, alluring, fascinating, or even only had the possibility of being so, found in that message his reason for being. And that reason for being was certain because it was a *presence*. It gave one hope that everything could be embraced. In that moment he found an answer to my friend in the university. Giussani found the one who could keep every beautiful thing that happened in life. Everything that was beautiful was made to keep forever.

An historical event like this introduces a newness that, even after 60 years, he remembers as the crucial moment. It's like the Gospel of John itself. John met Jesus, and 60 years later he wrote the Gospel, remembering the moment, the place, the hour in which that event happened. This is the significant event, the Person who introduced the change that Pope Benedict speaks of. This is what we are looking for. An event that is not the result of an effort, that we can recognize as something we are incapable of doing, something that can sustain us every day of our life. But it is something that shapes our life in such a way that, from this moment on, the instant is no longer trivial. Everything is full of density, of intensity, of warmness, everything is full of meaning. This is the promise of Christianity as an event.

Cameron: Is it possible for this event to be something stable in our life?

Carrón: Yes, it's possible if we recognize that it's something *given*. That it's not something we can create with our energy, with our forces. What is the only possibility of keeping this newness? Only by receiving it continuously. This newness is such a gift, that only if we are in touch with the origin of this event, this history, can this event become more and more stable in our lives, because we are always taking part in this event. The question is to identify the origin. This origin is not an idea on ethics or an effort, because this origin is a place, a living reality in which this keeps happening. The newness we seek is in this place. This is our Christian community, really alive. This is the way in which we can participate in this newness. This is what Christ promised to us, "I will be with you until the end of the world." Well, He is with us until the end of the world. Where? In a place, in a living reality that is the life of the Church. We can be reawakened in our life, and in this being reawakened, we can participate in a stable way in this newness because we are constantly receiving this newness.

Cameron: And as a final question, Fr. Carrón, can you tell us in a few words what this new life would look like?

Carrón: If we allow Christ to enter into our heart, He will become our companion in the adventure of life. His presence will determine the sentiment of ourselves, as a beloved person will determine our perception of life. We Christians are not visionary people. We are not seeing things that are not there. We meet people changed by this event. Not visionary people. A person who falls in love is not a visionary. He is in touch with somebody, a real person. He is not simply alone in the relationship with reality. This companionship of Christ allows us to see reality in a more complete and entire way. I want to give an example. A boy is able to look at reality better when he is in the company of his parents. This example came to me when I was teaching high school. If a boy is visiting Disneyland with his family, he is happy and glad, because everything strikes him. Everything is a surprise. He's curious. He's enjoying every attraction that he sees with his eyes. He enjoys every attraction of the park. But if in a moment of distraction he gets lost in the middle of the park, all the attraction remains there, everything is just beautiful as before, but everything would be perceived by this boy in a different way. What earlier had been regarded positively all of a sudden becomes strange because he is alone and full of fear. Having gotten lost, everything all of a sudden becomes a menace, something to introduce fear in him. The moment he finds his family again, everything changes back to perfection. The attractions recovers their beauty. Beauty prevails over menace. And the boy starts to enjoy everything again. Recovering his adequate relationship with reality allows him to have a true perception of reality.

Living life in the company of Christ produces the same effect in our relationship with everything. Living life in His company, each thing becomes meaningful again. Time acquires sense, intensity, it's not empty anymore, but full of density. Nothing is banal, trivial, it's full of possibilities. Life becomes an adventure to enjoy together. What prevails is fascination, not boredom, even when the circumstances are challenging. Everything contains a promise. Wasting it would be a pity. Nothing is useless. Each thing is worthwhile. All this makes us free, even from the outcome. Reward is the action itself, as loving is the reward of love. We don't need to wait for something outside of love. We don't need confirmation outside of the experience itself. Everything is inside of this experience. We become free. This makes us free from the circumstances surrounding us. Even inside adverse circumstances we are not dependent on them. That is our dream. Not depending on every circumstance. We want to know in the deepest part of ourselves that we are not determined by them. We are human beings. We are lord, not slave, of the circumstances. Christ's companionship generates a capacity for affection for ourselves which is beyond imagination. No other company is able to awaken such an affection for ourselves. Tenderness towards ourselves finally becomes a reality. No blame can prevail. No mistake or failure is able to overcome its power. His presence prevails over everything. His presence allows us, finally, to reconcile our inner desires. Often people get angry with their own needs of fulfillment. They are too weak for human energy. No effort or strategy reaches to answer them. Their claims are beyond human possibility of achievement. This is the greatness of the human being, but frequently human desires become a condemnation because of the impossibility of answering them. Only if we find Who is capable of fulfilling them can we make possible a real affection for our own nature, for our real self.

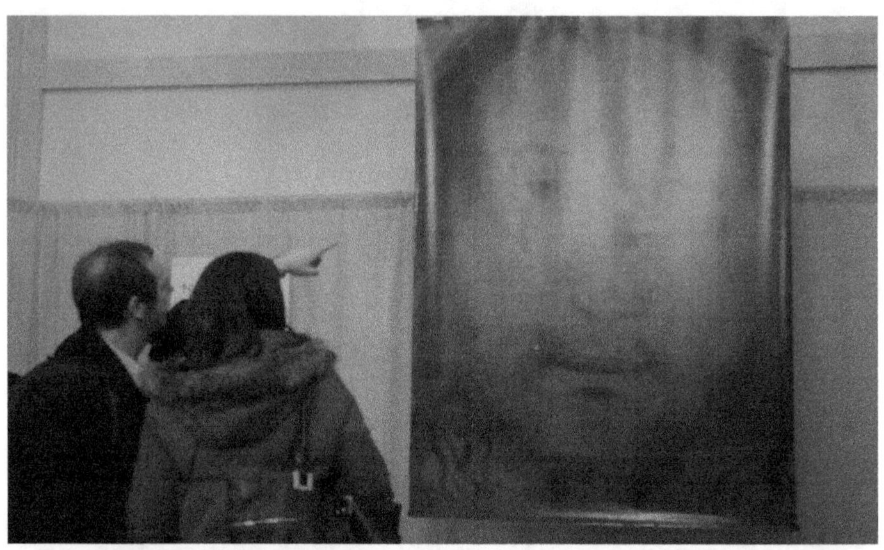

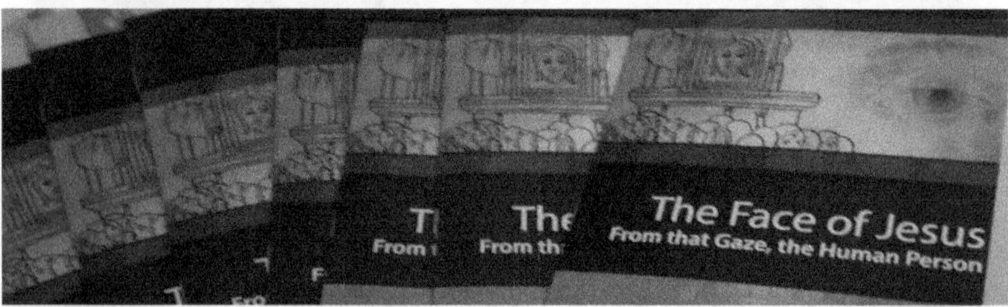
The Face of Jesus
From that Gaze, the Human Person

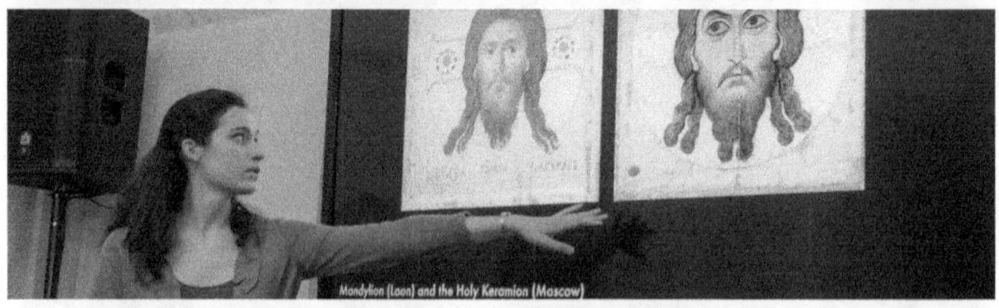
Mandylion (Laon) and the Holy Keramion (Moscow)

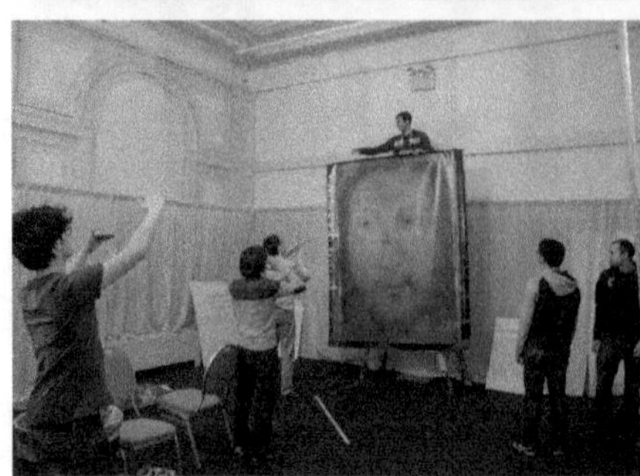

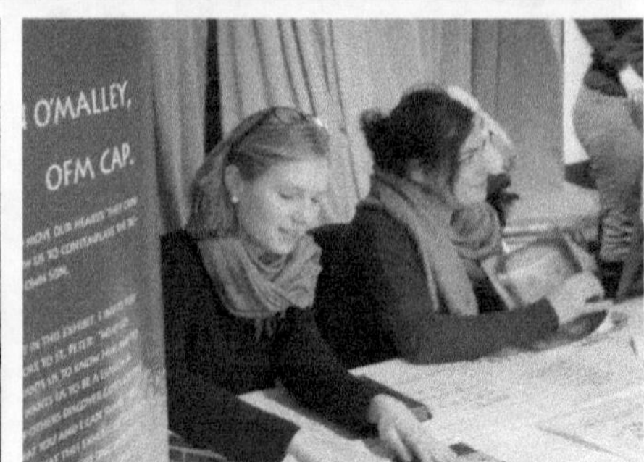
O'MALLEY,
OFM CAP.

Introduction to the Exhibit: "The Face of Jesus: From that Gaze, the Human Person"

Cardinal Seán O'Malley[1]

For us as Catholics, there is a long and sacred history of venerating the holy images of our Lord, Jesus Christ. At Christmastime, we incense the Holy Infant in the manger and recall His humility and love. During Lent we walk with devotion through the Stations of the Cross, tracing the steps that lead to our salvation. And on Easter morning we stand before the empty tomb, filled with awe in the presence of the Angels at the wondrous works that God has done. Images of Christ have the power to move our hearts, they can catechize without words and allow us to contemplate the beautiful face of God revealed in His own Son.

Images of Christ are also signs for the Church on pilgrimage. As pilgrims, we know that we walk through this world with our eyes "fixed on Jesus" (cf. Heb 12:2), so that He may be for us the "Way, the Truth, and the Life" (cf. John 14:6). Throughout the centuries, Jesus' face has been depicted in a number of different ways. At times He is depicted as the one who suffers in His Passion, out of love for humanity. At other times He is shown as the one who teaches and who invites disciples to follow Him. And there are still other depictions of Christ in Glory, bearing the wounds of His Passion as a sign of His love and proof of His sacrifice for us. These images are all meant to accompany us in life and give us hope and strength.

When I was a child, they used to read to us the story about a king who was a good man. He decided he would disguise himself as a peasant so that he could go and live amongst his subjects. He wanted to experience their suf-

Sunday, January 19, 2014

[1]Archbishop of Boston

ferings and know their aspirations. As moving as this story might be, the Incarnation of the Son of God is quite different. In the Incarnation, Jesus does not come disguised as one of us but He comes as one of us, a brother. He does not come to get to know us. He comes so we can get to know Him, our God. He is the revelation. He is the event. He has not come for a short visit but to insert Himself into our history permanently. He is with us. He is our contemporary.

Fr. Giussani's charism was to help so many young people discover Christ in their lives. It is in the Church, in communion, that we have the best opportunity to experience Christ and His friendship. The poison of our contemporary culture is the extreme individualism of the age, which is documented in Professor Putnam's study on Americans, *Bowling Alone*,[1] in which Putnam demonstrates how each generation of Americans is becoming more and more isolated, more and more alienated. There are more people living alone, eating alone, and spending hours before a television screen or computer alone. In His Incarnation, God is with us and will never abandon us. He comes to take us out of our isolation and invites us into true friendship and communion.

As we look upon the face of Christ in this exhibit, I invite you to meditate on those words He spoke to St. Peter: "Who do you say that I am?" (Luke 9:20). He wants us to know Him and to know how much He loves us. He wants us to be a leaven in our world, a light that will help others discover God's presence, His Love and His Beauty, so that you and I can share that with the whole community. I pray that this exhibit of the face of Christ will draw those who look upon it to discover in it the face of love and mercy, the face of the One who calls us to follow Him.

---

[1]Robert D. Putnam, *Bowling Alone,* New York: Simon & Schuster, 2000.

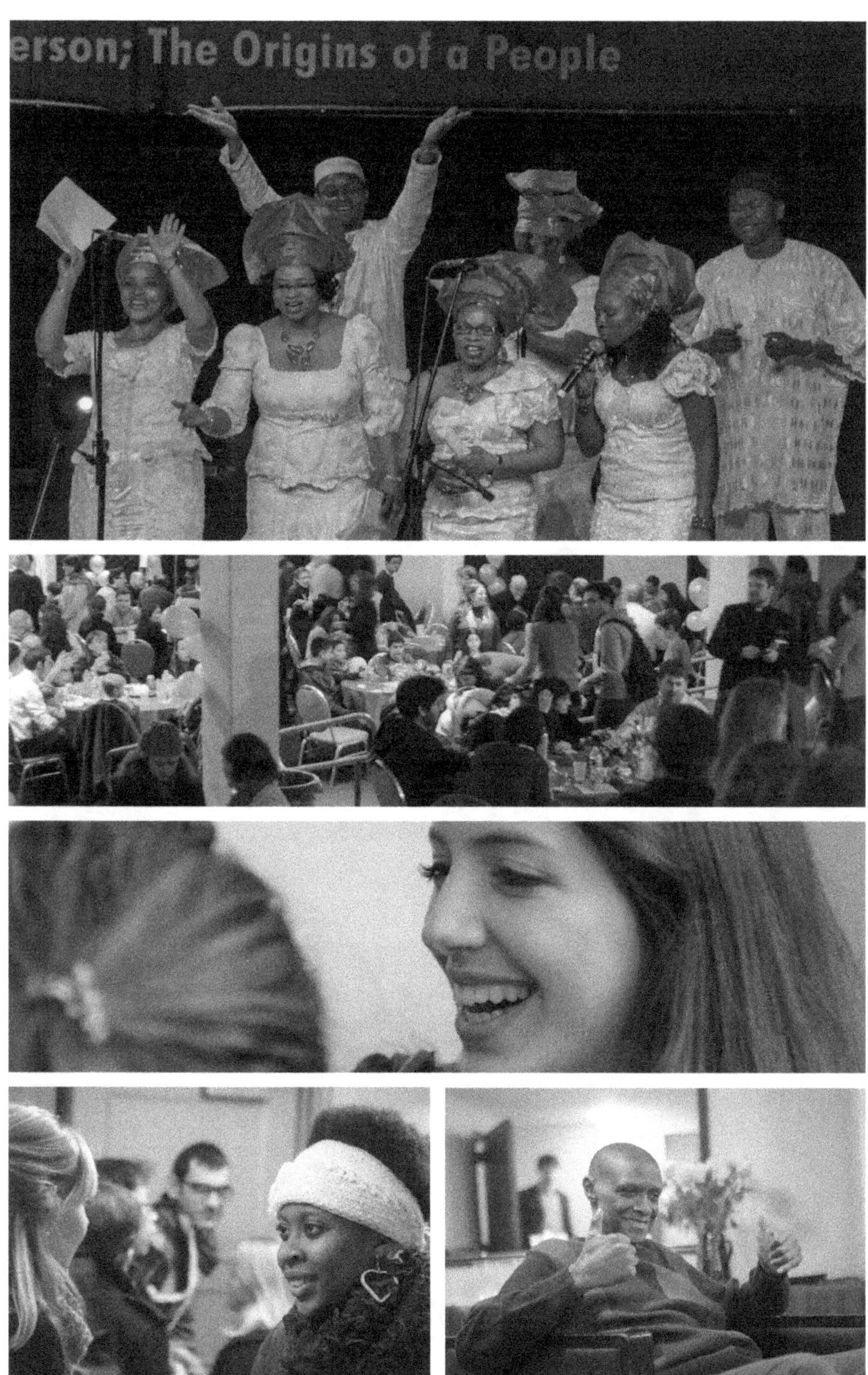
erson; The Origins of a People

NEW YORK ENCOUNTER

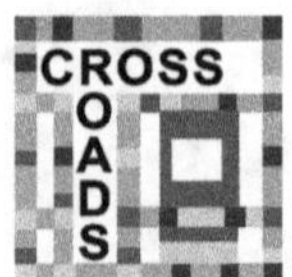

Crossroads Cultural Center

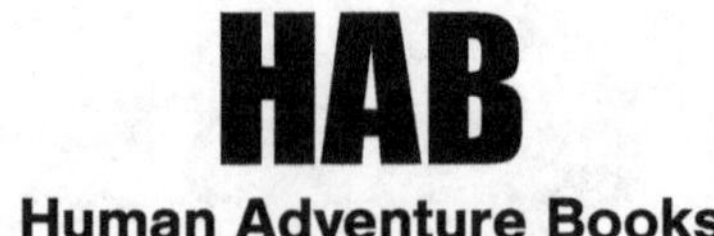

www.ingramcontent.com/pod-product-compliance
Lightning Source LLC
LaVergne TN
LVHW010101110826
845155LV00028B/442